YOU'RE NOT THAT SPECIAL

Ditch the Myth, Face the Truth, and
Build Unstoppable Momentum

YOU'RE NOT THAT SPECIAL

MARY AJAYI

Library of Congress Cataloging-in-Publication Data

Ajayi, Mary.

You're Not That Special: Ditch the Myth, Face the Truth, and Build Unstoppable Momentum / Mary Ajayi.—1st ed.

1. Self-actualization (Psychology). 2. Motivation (Psychology). 3. Personal Growth. I. Title.

Hardcover ISBN: 979-8-9989516-0-2
Paperback ISBN: 979-8-9989516-2-6
E-book ISBN: 979-8-9989516-3-3

Library of Congress Control Number (LCCN): 2025911799

First Edition, November 2025

Printed in the United States of America

10 9 8 7 6 5 4 3 2 1

To the overthinkers, over-preparers, and almost-doers.

This is your invitation to begin.

Contents

The Wake-Up Call

"The way to get started is to quit talking and begin doing."

—WALT DISNEY

For years, I clung to the notion that I was destined to stand out, that I was part of an elite minority whose unique spark would eventually propel me beyond the ordinary, not because of an endless workload or an insatiable ambition, nor because I had an exceptional ability or brilliance. I believed I was inherently special, carrying an unspoken energy that set me apart. I imagined that every sign, from the stars in the sky to the subtle hints in everyday life, was orchestrating my eventual rise, a quiet signal that my moment was coming.

Like many of you, I, too, pictured a future when success would quietly reveal itself, gently tap me on the shoulder, and confirm that I was destined for greatness. I never spoke these beliefs aloud, but deep down, I nurtured the comforting myth of being extraordinary. I secretly hoped that some external force would one day fix all my flaws and an unseen hand would perfect what I felt was missing.

And so, I waited. In that waiting, I dressed up my inaction with kinder names: "alignment" for procrastination, "patience" for hesitation, and "processing" for fear. I convinced myself I wasn't stuck; I was evolving, even if it seemed imperceptibly slow. I dreamed of a day when each piece of my life would effortlessly fall into place and all today's struggles seamlessly transitioned into tomorrow's triumphs.

Then reality made itself clear. It wasn't a dramatic breakdown or a moment of crisis that shattered my illusion. It was an ordinary day when I looked around and recognized that nothing had changed. The same excuses and inertia persisted. New goals appeared, but I remained mired in the familiar cycle of inaction.

That day, I understood that neither you nor I are inherently special. I share this truth not to deflate you but to free you from the myth of exceptionalism. The moment I stopped waiting for a magical sign and instead chose to act marked the beginning of a genuine transformation. I stopped waiting for confidence to appear; I began building it step by step. I ceased seeking external validation and instead made decisions that propelled me forward.

If you're still reading these words, you've likely experienced that paralyzing pause, that stubborn feeling of being stuck. Perhaps you've mastered the art of presenting progress: curating Pinterest boards, journaling methodically, listening to endless motivational podcasts, and reciting affirmations. You seem prepared and insightful.

Yet beneath that polished surface, you remain in limbo. You scrutinize every opportunity, hesitate at challenges cloaked as caution, and churn out plans that never take action. You tell yourself you're waiting for more clarity, a few more moments, additional preparation. Deep down, you know this waiting is precisely what held you back.

Stuck ≠ Confusion

The truth is simple: you aren't stuck because you're confused. You're stuck because you've been sold the idea that you're an exception to the rules of consistent action and disciplined growth.

You've been led to believe that your timing is unique and that your struggles are not your problem. But that mindset may be the barrier that keeps you trapped in a circle of self-doubt. We've all been told to "trust the timing" without learning how to distinguish real readiness from fear dressed up as destiny.

Consider the messages you've received: You are already enough, deserve success by merely existing, and the right opportunities will eventually appear. While these ideas have appeal, they come with a hidden caveat. They suggest that growth comes from a sense of inherent worth rather than through hard work and that clarity will come before action. Growth is not a waiting game; clarity and confidence are byproducts of consistent, deliberate action.

This book isn't here to coddle you. It's here to cut through the excuses. You don't need an overnight transformation; you need to start behaving as someone who's done waiting. Here is the hard truth: you won't gain momentum by passively consuming podcasts or waiting for that elusive moment of divine insight; momentum is created through continuous, deliberate effort. And that is precisely what this book offers: a no-nonsense, actionable roadmap designed to shift you from hesitation to decisive action.

What's Inside:

■ **Part 1:** Exposes the deceptions you've been living under, like your persistent belief in your notable exception and the myth of the "right time."

■ **Part 2:** Introduces the REAL Method, a practical framework for Recognizing your habits, exposing your fears, acting with determination, and locking in proactive routines that drive progress.

■ **Part 3:** Focuses on building genuine confidence, not by chasing perfection or expecting to be fearless, but by cultivating consistency through small, intentional steps.

■ **Part 4:** Shares real-life transformations and practical advice on overcoming setbacks with resilience rather than stagnating.

■ **Part 5:** Equips you with the tools to maintain your newly gained momentum; offering strategies to build resilience, safeguard progress, and prepare for life's inevitable challenges.

Throughout the book, you'll find concise chapters, bold soundbites, reflective prompts, and practical tools that push you into immediate action. This isn't a book meant to be admired from a distance; it's a helpful guide meant to jolt you into motion. It challenges you to confront your current habits, take responsibility, and begin a process of gradual but dedicated reformation. You can make a change, and this book is your tool.

This book is not about making excuses for inaction or dwelling on brokenness. It's about recognizing your potential and taking control of your destiny. A breakthrough isn't waiting for you to feel fully ready; it begins when you decide to act.

Clarity is earned, confidence is built, and action is the quickest path to change.

This book is structured to reverse the common trap of waiting for clarity before you act. Instead, you'll find guidance on moving forward and allow clarity to follow naturally. Every section is clear and purposeful; no fluff, no filler. Each sentence is designed to encourage you to act. You will encounter tough-love chapter titles, assertive sound-bites, thought-provoking prompts, and practical tools that compel you to take action. If you're ready to stop spinning your wheels and begin real progress, it's time to reclaim your momentum in five transformative parts.

Author's Note:

Many of the stories and coaching scenarios in this book are drawn from real experiences; my own and those of people I've worked with over the years. To respect their privacy, names and specific details have been altered. The shared truths of struggle, turning points, and powerful steps toward change remain. Your journey of transformation is just as real and within reach.

Let's get to work.

01

THE LIES YOU TELL YOURSELF

"

ALWAYS REMEMBER THAT YOU ARE ABSOLUTELY UNIQUE. JUST LIKE EVERYONE ELSE.

—MARGARET MEAD

"

CHAPTER 1

You're Not Special, And That's Good News

The First Lie I Ever Believed

I can't pinpoint the exact moment I began to buy into the idea I was different from others, but I know it didn't happen all at once. It wasn't the result of a single comment or an earth-shattering revelation that swept over me with sudden intensity. Instead, it was a slow and steady drip of seemingly insignificant moments: small affirmations and gentle acknowledgments that eventually took root. Quiet praises, well-meaning compliments, and little gestures of approval collected and settled into my bones, becoming part of me.

"You're so mature for your age," a teacher casually remarked when I was 12.

"You're going to do big things," an uncle proclaimed at a family dinner.

"You're gifted," a mentor declared in a letter that felt like a seal of promise.

These words were more than just expressions of kindness: they were powerful narratives that shaped my identity. They built a framework, a complete story I carried with me, unexamined and unchallenged. Before I knew it, I wasn't merely believing in my potential; I was relying on it. I was expecting it to carry me forward and do the heavy lifting.

That expectation quietly rewired my thinking until it became my default setting. I operated under the assumption that things would naturally fall into place because I was "special." I thought my life's path would be smoother and more meaningful than that of others, untouched by ordinary struggles and setbacks.

I never said these things out loud, never voiced them because I didn't need to. A silent certainty brewed within me, a steady assurance that my story would unfold differently from most, not due to any particular actions, but simply because of who I believed I was. I waited for the spark, for that moment of revelation, expecting the switch to flip at any second.

In the meantime, I worked hard in theory, planning, journaling, strategizing, learning, but it was all abstract. I wasn't moving forward; I circled my goals, orbiting them endlessly without ever landing. My potential felt like a promise, a strong force that was supposed to propel me, but instead, it was keeping me stuck. It was a paradox. It empowered me and trapped me.

The EV Charger App Dream

I've always been drawn to beginnings: that first spark of an idea, the thrill of late-night Google dives, the endless rabbit holes waiting to be explored.

Years ago, long before electric vehicles showed up at every charging plaza, I pictured grocery store parking lots dotted with chargers like gas stations line highways. But I didn't stop at stations. I wanted to build an app showing you where chargers were, which were free, and how long you'd wait.

I sketched wireframes on napkins, ran numbers in spreadsheets, and drafted a basic data-flow diagram for real-time availability. It felt urgent, inevitable... until the questions arrived:

- How would I get real-time data?

- Would store chains let me install hardware?

- Who would fund it?

- Was I even qualified to tackle enterprise-level contracts?

So, I did what many of us do when we're afraid to move forward: I sought validation instead of clarity. I shared the concept with friends and family; polite nods, no momentum. Then, I pitched it to my boyfriend at the time, hoping for encouragement. Instead, he grilled me:

"How will you get APIs from multiple providers? Who's covering liability if someone's car dies? Have you mapped out a revenue model?"

Each question was fair, but I wasn't prepared with answers. Rather than treat it as a challenge, I shut down. I quit before I started.

Now, whenever I drive past a Walmart and see half a dozen apps offering live charger maps, real-time wait times, and integrated payment, my throat tightens, not because someone else succeeded, but because I never gave myself a chance.

And it wasn't a one-off. I scrolled past job listings I was perfectly qualified for, whispering "Not me" before my thumb hit "next." I ignored podcast invites, declined conference panels, ghosted DMs, convinced my story wasn't worth hearing or terrified it would expose me as a fraud.

I drafted business plans for a bistro and a beverage line, domains bought, mood boards assembled, but never launched. I was always planning, never doing. Once, I rehearsed an introduction so obsessively that I arrived at the networking event after it ended.

I wasn't afraid of failure. I feared visibility, taking up space with an idea that didn't promise instant success. So, I stayed locked in my head, waiting for that mythical moment when I'd feel "ready." **Spoiler:** it never came.

I've learned that readiness isn't a destination; it's the first step you take toward the unknown. If you wait for perfect conditions, you'll always be standing still.

 You ever have that one drawer in your room filled with beautiful outfits you never wear? Clothes you swore you'd rock when the occasion felt "right"? That's how most people treat their potential. Always tucked away. Always waiting for the perfect day.

Meanwhile, life's happening in sweatpants.

That drawer gets fuller. Dustier. And eventually, you stop opening it. Not because the clothes stopped fitting; but because you stopped believing they were yours to wear.

The belief that I was special didn't lead to early success or clarity as I had imagined it would. Instead, it left me feeling immobilized, filled with uncertainty and anxiety. It was as if I were on a train that I didn't have to drive, only to realize it was traveling in circles without a clear destination. It was unsettling, this gap between who I was and who I was supposed to be.

I felt I was missing a puzzle piece, but I couldn't name it. Friends moved forward, leaping into first jobs, relationships, and adventures while I lingered, waiting for something spectacular to happen, something that always felt out of reach. The more I waited, the more anxious I became. I started to fear that all the affirmations and predictions were merely illusions. What if I was never special? What if I'd been telling myself a lie all along?

The Myth of Being Special

The notion that you are special is not the flattering compliment you might imagine it to be. In reality, it's a cunning trap deceptively gilded with allure. While on the surface, it appears to be empowering, it is, in fact, a velvet cage that gently lulls you into a state of inaction, offering the deceitful promise of a smoother, obstacle-free journey through life. This sense of specialness whispers sweetly in your ear, telling you that there's no need to start from scratch, no necessity to face the struggles and trials that everyone else encounters. It suggests that your life's path will be markedly different, for your destiny is supposedly unique and untouched by the mundane challenges others face. This seductive lie feels truthful precisely because it is so comforting. It assures you that success will occur. Naturally, that opportunity will serendipitously seek you out, and you are somehow exempt from the relentless grind that characterizes the pursuit of achievement.

However, this sense of specialness is just entitlement cloaked in an appealing guise. It fosters a subtle arrogance within you, the quiet assumption that the ordinary rules and limitations do not apply to someone with your perceived uniqueness. You expect that your learning curve will be shorter and less arduous, your ideas will naturally stand out without requiring significant effort, and your timeline for success will be expedited compared to others. You may begin to regard consistency as a trait necessary only for those who lack your grand "vision," and you may view struggle as something beneath your supposed "potential." Consequently, when life becomes complicated, and you feel lost in the chaos, overwhelmed by the weight of it all, or achingly average, you find yourself unable to take action. Instead, you spiral into doubt and uncertainty. You hesitate and wait, paralyzed by the belief that your journey was meant to be different. Somewhere along the way, someone led you to believe that being special meant you would be spared life's ordinary, mundane challenges and sold you on the myth that your path should be an effortless triumph.

REALITY CHECK

Everyone is unique, yet no one is born with a special privilege to bypass hard work. You're not exceptionally different, nor is the person beside you, whether in line, on your preferred podcast, or on television. This is positive because it indicates that the difference between someone struggling and someone succeeding isn't fate; it's about choosing to take action instead of waiting for a miracle.

Now, let's explore why this myth seems so alluring...

The Psychology Behind It

Let's take a closer look at the mechanics of this lie. The desire to feel special is rooted in one of the most fundamental human needs: the need for significance. We all long for validation and a sense of meaning, believing that our pain, stories, and ideas carry more importance than they sometimes do. This need breathes life into the myth of specialness, making us feel that we are destined for something greater and that our struggles are imbued with singular weight. It's comforting to imagine we are here for something monumental. However, the reality is that when this search for significance isn't anchored in tangible action, it becomes tenuous and brittle. This unmet need begins to morph into toxic patterns that serve only to ensnare you: perfectionism that paralyzes you before you even start, persistent overthinking masquerading as strategy, unnecessary delays masquerading as "planning," or a sense of victimhood cunningly framed as authenticity. These are not simply personality quirks; they are the traps that keep you from moving forward.

This is precisely where the exceptionalism bias sneaks in, a cognitive phenomenon well-documented in behavioral science. It convinces you, quite erroneously, that the world's rules somehow do not apply to you in the same way they apply to everyone else. This bias creeps in quietly and comfortably, manifesting in small but significant ways. You might find yourself assuming that you'll master new skills in record time or that your groundbreaking idea will instantly stand out from the crowd without any real effort. You may even begin to think that consistency, a trait proven essential for success, is only necessary for those who are less "gifted." The brutal irony is this: the more you succumb to these beliefs, the less likely you are to succeed. Don't take my word for it; countless studies on habit formation and behavior change support this conclusion. They've repeatedly shown that meaningful, long-term transformation does not result from sheer intensity or isolated instances of brilliance. Instead, it stems from dull, often tedious consistency. The individuals who achieve real, lasting growth are not those who anticipate an easy ride. They are the ones who embrace the monotony of repetition, who bravely endure the mundane steps most of us choose to avoid.

When you've bought into the belief that you're special, consistency begins to feel beneath you, almost like an insult to your imagined potential. You start chasing shortcuts, waiting indefinitely for moments of clarity, or endlessly hunting for inspiration, hoping you'll "show up when it matters." You devote your energy not to building systems that function but to perfecting plans that remain theoretical. And the longer you persist in this cycle of waiting, the more disconnected you become from the practical actions that would genuinely propel you forward. This is not a problem of laziness; it's one of fear: a fear of being average, of not standing out, of enduring the hard but necessary struggles, and, most importantly, of shattering the cherished fantasy of effortless success. Unlike those who embrace consistency to succeed, you end up waiting in fear and missing out on growth.

Being told you're special creates a dangerously seductive illusion. It feels like an unexpected gift wrapped in a bow and delivered straight to your sense of self-worth. But it's a lousy tool for real, meaningful change. This belief pulls your focus inward to fixate on your identity, self-perception, and supposed uniqueness when actual progress demands outward action and effort. The mirage of specialness constructs an unspoken rulebook that stifles growth: you shouldn't have to start small; you should learn faster than others, and you certainly don't need the structure that limits the less gifted. You are left waiting interminably for the future, perfected version of yourself to arrive on the scene fully formed, fearless, and ready to take on everything you've been postponing. But that future self isn't coming. It never was. The reality is that the only version of you that exists is the one who can act today, and today, you don't care in the slightest how special you think you are. It only cares whether or not you take steps to move.

This false sense of specialness makes you fragile, even more so than you might imagine. When your identity becomes tied up in being exceptional, every little setback feels like an existential crisis. A product launch flops, and rather than see it as a learning experience, you immediately wonder if you're not cut out for this. A social media post gets no likes, and instead of reconsidering your strategy, you assume you're not meant to be seen. A rejection letter arrives, and your entire sense of potential collapses. You question your worth, your abilities, and your whole life trajectory. But what if these experiences of being ignored, unseen, and underwhelming are just the normal start of every great endeavor? What if this is how all substantial effort begins, and specialness is the only thing getting in your way? What if being ordinary is the reasonable tax you pay for extraordinary?

Let me tell you about someone who embraced being ordinary and found herself....

My artist friend spent years on the cusp of greatness, or so she believed. She had talent, a rare gift for capturing light and emotion, but she waited for the world to validate her genius. Every project had to be a masterpiece. She'd start a painting, see a flaw, and discard it in frustration. She became convinced that true brilliance would emerge only when some magical alignment happened: the perfect studio, the right inspiration, a sudden spark of insight. But those conditions never arrived. Instead, she found herself drowning in half-finished work and self-doubt.

Eventually, she got so fed up that she decided to prove her inadequacy once and for all. She committed to finishing 50 small paintings in 50 days, expecting them to confirm her fears. The first few were awkward, stilted, and painful to complete. But each day, she kept going. When something didn't turn out, she moved on to the next canvas without pausing to compare it to her impossible standards. By the end of the challenge, she'd made more art than in all the years she'd waited for perfection.

What amazed her most was how many pieces she truly loved. Flaws she'd once considered insurmountable became part of her style. She realized she didn't need permission to create; she only needed to accept the messiness of the process. And in that mess, she found freedom.

The lesson here is simple but profound: if you wait to feel special before you act, you'll wait forever. The key isn't to believe you're extraordinary. It's to act as if you're ordinary and let action make you exceptional. When you do something consistently (write, paint, start a business), you release the pressure of specialness and embrace the power of progress. You treat setbacks as experiments instead of verdicts on your identity. You find strength in the mundane discipline of showing up. And in doing so, you might surprise yourself.

So, what's the "real" secret to creative success? It's not being special. It's getting comfortable with the uncomfortable process of growth. It's committing to action, even when you don't feel ready. It's embracing failure as a sign you're on the right track. The only thing standing between you and your best work isn't talent or timing. It's the decision to start before you're ready.

It's supposed to be hard. It's supposed to feel clumsy, like a language you've just begun to learn. The discomfort is the process, not the problem. When you expect it, you're less likely to give up. Embrace this phase. If you can sit with the urge to quit and let the messiness exist without rushing to fix it, you're on your way. This isn't settling; it is how you grow.

Most people can't handle the awkward, honest beginning. They get anxious and quit before the compounding kicks in. Don't be most people. If you stay, you win. You'll outlast the doubt and the desire to skip to a polished end. And what you'll find is that there's freedom in being unremarkable. If you're not special, you have nothing to lose. You can try, fail, and try again without the pressure of perfection. You can adapt. You can learn. You can excel, gradually, at being consistent.

The Gift of Failure

Failure is underrated. It shows you what doesn't work, clearing the way for what might. It forces you off the path of least resistance and into the territory where real innovation happens. When you stop seeing failure as a flaw, you start to see it as a gift: a reminder that you're doing something that matters, something worth the risk.

Most people never get here. They're so afraid of failing that they never really start. They tinker, they daydream, they wait for assurance. But assurance never comes. Failure is the only way. It's the currency you pay for progress. Learn to fail better, and it's the best investment ever. Pile up enough failures, and you'll look up one day to see you've succeeded.

FRAMEWORK: **THE REAL STARTING POINT**

To know if you're ready to move or just pretending to be productive, use this mental model: **The REAL Test.** Ask yourself:

■ **R:** Am I Repeating the same prep loop? Reading, researching, planning again?

■ **E:** Am I Emotionally attached to being seen as talented? Is my identity tied to how others view my potential?

■ **A:** Am I Avoiding beginner steps because they feel beneath me? Do I think starting small is for others?

■ **L:** Am I Lying to myself about not being ready? Am I using "preparation" as an excuse for fear?

If you say **yes** to any of these, you're not being strategic: you're being scared. That's okay but call it what it is. Naming the lie is the first step to dismantling it. Fear is normal. Letting it masquerade as strategy isn't.

REFLECTION PROMPT: **YOUR FAVORITE COMFORTING LIE**

Take two minutes and write down the most believable excuse you've been using to delay action. Maybe it's "I'm not ready," "I need more clarity," or "I'll start when the timing's right."

Be honest.

Now answer:

1.   What feeling does this excuse protect you from? Fear of failure? Embarrassment? Being seen as average?

....

....

....

2.   What identity does it let you keep? The visionary? The perfectionist? The "gifted" one?

....

....

....

3.   What would happen if you acted anyway? What's the smallest step you could take today?

....

....

....

This isn't about shaming yourself. It's about seeing the story you've been telling yourself and choosing a new one.

What's Coming Next?

This chapter is your initial, daring step into genuine action. Now that you're embracing the uncomfortable, it's time to dispel another myth: you must be fully prepared before you start. We've bought into the comforting lie that we can only move when ready, but the truth is that readiness reveals itself along the journey. It unfolds with each uncertain step, not a neat package you possess beforehand.

In the next chapter, we'll dive into the psychological game of potential and why it feels so compelling yet proves hazardous to real growth. We'll explore how this seductive focus on what **could** be keeps you from what **is,** and why the allure of endless possibility traps you in perpetual stagnation. You'll learn to break free from this alluring but paralyzing loop and transform potential into palpable progress.

I'll introduce you to a simple and effective system that stops you from circling in endless preparation and begins stacking tangible change. It's a framework designed to shift your mindset and actions, turning vague visions into concrete accomplishments. This system will reveal how to create and sustain momentum, allowing you to bypass the seductive call of perfection and dive directly into impactful, transformative work. You'll discover how to start with what you have and let growth follow rather than waiting for some imagined distant readiness. Action, we'll find, is the true catalyst for clarity, not the other way around.

But before we get there, let's take a moment to reflect on your current patterns. Consider the stories you've been telling yourself: those comforting, convincing narratives that have delayed your progress. How have these tales kept you in a state of non-action? What excuses seem most believable and reassuring, and what feelings are they protecting you from facing?

This reflection will set the foundation for the changes to come. It will help you see how you've been unintentionally holding yourself back and prepare you to turn those insights into forward momentum.

The Lie of Being Special

We're told from a young age that we're special: that we have unique gifts and talents, and it's meant to build us up but can trap us instead. If you're special, it means the world owes you something: recognition, praise, and ease. You wonder what went wrong when those things didn't come as quickly or easily as expected. You think you've failed because life isn't matching your story. You question your gifts when the world doesn't recognize them instantly.

But here's the liberating truth: you're not special. Not in the way you were told. There's freedom in that. It means you're not entitled to anything, so you're not failing if you don't have everything yet. It means that the gap between you and the life you want isn't a flaw in you but a bridge you get to build. Consistency fills it. Effort fills it. Work fills it.

The Life You Want Is Boring

We imagine the life we want as wild and exhilarating. We think achieving our dreams will be constant fireworks, thrills, and amazement. But here's the reality: the life you want is boring. It's routine. It's small steps taken again and again, day after day. Writers write for hours in solitude. Entrepreneurs send a hundred emails that go unanswered. Artists paint the same scene a hundred times to get it right.

When you accept that and stop expecting every day to be epic, you free yourself to live the life you want. You stop bailing when things get tedious. You stop quitting when things aren't instantly rewarding. You realize the work is the reward.

The process is supposed to feel mind-numbingly routine. It's supposed to test your patience like hours in a waiting room, stretching forever. It's supposed to be ordinary, full of unspectacular tasks that you repeat, uncelebrated, hoping they eventually stack up into something meaningful. But there's a hidden blessing in that because waiting for your work to feel special keeps you from doing the work. When you expect to feel like a rockstar every day, you're setting yourself up to quit. Accepting that the life you want is mostly a collection of unspectacular moments, you've permitted yourself to build it. You've released yourself from the pressure of fireworks, excitement, and constant amazement and committed to something better: the discipline to keep showing up.

> Once you accept that the life you want is boring, you can finally get on with living it.

That acceptance frees you. You stop bailing when things get tedious; instead, you dig into the tedium with an understanding that it's where the good stuff grows. You stop quitting the minute things aren't instantly rewarding; instead, you let the rewards come in their own time. You redefine success from shiny and instant to lasting, built on the pillars of consistency and time. The process is the reward. In embracing it, you'll find yourself sticking with the things you once abandoned. You'll find yourself achieving what you once thought was out of reach.

You'll find that the secret to the success you want isn't talent, luck, or timing but the ability to love the boring stuff enough to stick with it. And that's where the magic happens.

FRAMEWORK: **THE ANTI-SPECIAL SYSTEM**

Let's build your first system: The Anti-Special System. It's designed to get you out of your head and into motion with three principles:

- **Track what you do, not how you feel.** Stop using mood as a measure. Did you write? Move? Reach out? That's what counts.

- **Shrink the starting line.** Don't wait for a perfect day. What's the 5-minute version of what you're putting off? 100 words, one email, a short walk.

- **Stack the reps, not the results.** Progress compounds when you show up consistently, not when the outcome arrives. You don't need a big win; you need small steps, over and over.

This is how ordinary people build extraordinary lives— not by feeling destined but by being consistent in the unseen moments.

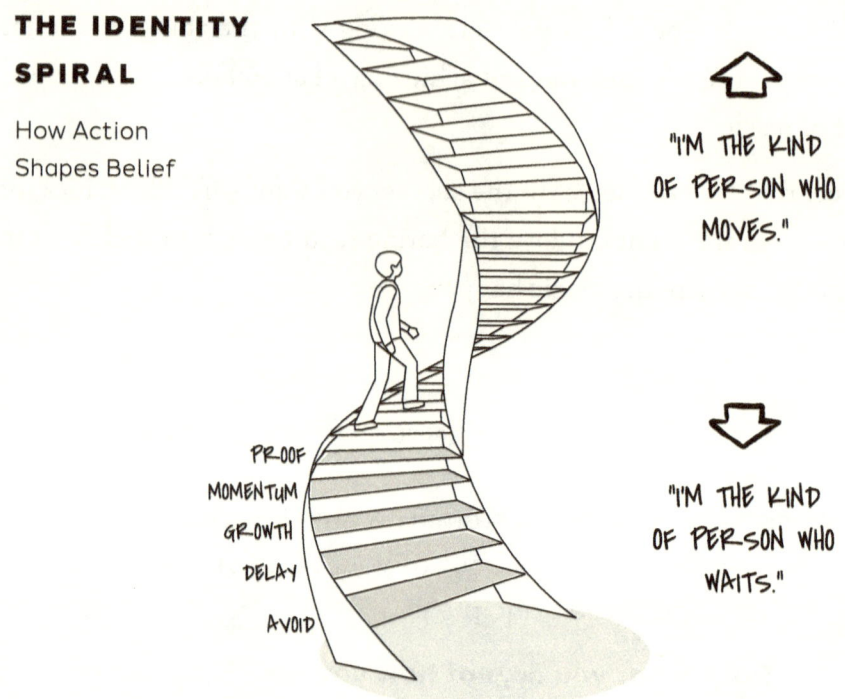

THE IDENTITY SPIRAL

How Action
Shapes Belief

PROOF
MOMENTUM
GROWTH
DELAY
AVOID

"I'M THE KIND OF PERSON WHO MOVES."

"I'M THE KIND OF PERSON WHO WAITS."

Imagine your identity as a spiral staircase. Every action is a step, up or down. There's no standing still. When you show up, even for five minutes, you rise. You build proof: "I'm the kind of person who moves." When you delay, avoid, or rationalize, you descend, confirming: "I'm the kind of person who waits." The goal isn't to leap ten steps but to keep climbing, one imperfect action at a time. Momentum beats perfection. Do it today, not because it's impressive, but because it counts.

The most important step is the next one. Building the habit of action changes your relationship with success and failure. When you stop trying to be special, you can start to be curious. You're free to experiment, test, and learn. Suddenly, limitations are liberating. You don't need to know where you're headed. You only need to know where you're going right now. And right now, the only thing holding you back is the belief that you need to be great. Choose action over identity. Choose progress over self. You might surprise yourself.

Ritual Over Readiness

Replace readiness with ritual. Don't ask, "Do I feel like it?" Ask, "What's the next move I always take, no matter how I feel?" For me, it's a 90-second countdown timer. When I don't want to start, I set it and count it down. When it hits zero, I begin, not because I'm ready, but because I've trained myself to move. You can build your rituals: set your work shoes by the door, open your laptop before coffee, and keep your journal on your pillow. Make action obvious. Let repetition replace readiness.

ACTION PROMPT: **BUILD YOUR STARTING LINE**

Choose one area where you've been waiting for the spark: writing, fitness, content, speaking, boundaries, and self-discipline.

Define your Starting Line Rule:

"When I ___, I always do ___."

Examples:

- When I wake up, I always open my calendar.

- When I sit down, I always write for five minutes.

- When I open Instagram, I comment before I scroll.

Your brain craves habits. Replace hesitation with motion.

How Everyday Individuals Affect Remarkable Change

In my coaching group, I frequently observe individuals equipped with skills, ideas, and a domain name, yet they haven't taken the plunge.

■ **Jordan**, a cybersecurity student, was in this group. He had a well-prepared portfolio, a polished LinkedIn profile, and draft blog posts. However, he was stuck, fearing he would appear "unclear." I encouraged him to publish something within a week, even if it wasn't perfect. He ended up sharing a brief piece on cloud security. It garnered a few likes, a recruiter's message, and a peer's comment, "This helped me." This initial post became a weekly routine, building his confidence and opening new opportunities. Jordan didn't need perfection; he needed to begin.

■ **Taylor**, a graphic designer, spent months refining her portfolio, believing it wasn't "ready." I gave her the same challenge: share one piece this week. She posted a logo concept on Instagram. It wasn't her best work, but it received several likes and a collaboration request from a small business owner. That opportunity led to her first freelance client and, eventually, a steady stream of projects. Taylor didn't need to be flawless; she needed to be seen.

Growth Is A Process, Not A Destination.

We often confuse progress with identity, believing we must become entirely different before allowing ourselves to act in new or different ways. But that's not true. Your behaviors and actions pave the way for who you are, not the other way around. Each decision you make, no matter how it feels in the moment, is a building block in constructing the identity you wish to have. Want to be a writer? Then write.

Want to be fit? Start moving. Want to be confident? Decide to be. It's not a transformation that gets you started; it's the small steps. It's not an epiphany that prepares you; it's the systems that simplify taking action, making it second nature.

The way we think about change often traps us before we even begin. We need readiness, a marked shift in who we are. We wait for a magic moment when we suddenly feel different, transformed, and evolved. But growth is a process, not a destination. The life you want doesn't start when you become someone else; it begins when you take action as you are. The systems you build make those actions natural, obvious, and automatic. You don't need to change who you are to begin; you need to start to change who you are.

Why You Feel Stuck (And It's Not What You Think)

The biggest misconception is that you're stuck because you lack clarity or talent or feel lagging behind. In truth, you're stuck because you're trying to think your way into a new life instead of acting your way into one. Change is not a sudden revelation; it's a gradual process. You are frozen, not because something is fundamentally wrong, but because you're waiting for a spark when you should be cultivating a fire. You've been fixated on clarity when you should be establishing consistency, identifying too much with potential instead of creating systems to harness it, and idolizing your future self instead of engaging with your current self. You're not broken; you're just out of sync. And rhythm is something you can cultivate.

Your First Real System: R.I.S.E.

Here's a repeatable tool to snap you out of spiraling:

■ **R**ecognize your delay pattern. What do you do when avoiding action? Scroll? Overthink? Plan more? Name it.

■ **I**dentify your smallest next step. Not what's impressive; what gets the gears moving? An email? 200 words? A walk?

■ **S**implify the stakes. You're not building a legacy; you're typing a sentence, making a call, taking a step. Relax.

■ **E**xecute on a timer. Set for five minutes. Start. When the timer ends, stop or keep going.

It's simple because it works.

You don't need to be special to live your dream life. You don't even want to be. Clinging to that idea keeps you stuck because it makes you resist the things that genuinely change you. Special is a trickster who says, "It shouldn't be this hard." It pretends that those who succeed are especially suited for it, naturally gifted in a way you're not. But that's not true. The difference isn't natural talent; it's the systems they build. Those systems say, "I'll show up anyway." They say, "It's tough sometimes, and I am too." Special waits around, idle and hopeful, expecting the spark to simply appear. It wants the moment to feel right, not realizing it's those moments of waiting that hold you back. Systems don't wait. They stack the reps until the reps transform the process into second nature.

Special sits back and watches; it is passive. It's a bystander wondering why things aren't working out. Systems build momentum with repeated action; they are never still. Special wants dramatic urgency and fanfare before it starts; systems start small and keep moving because they know that's where progress lives. The magic happens independently when you fall in love with the systems and learn to trust them.

Above all, your systems, not any special moment, sustain you. Even if special moments come, they're fleeting. And momentum, small, unremarkable, daily, is what will carry you further than any exceptional moment ever could.

REFLECTION PROMPT: **WHERE HAVE I BEEN WAITING FOR READINESS**

Pause and write:

1. Where have I been waiting for readiness instead of building a system?

....

....

2. What identity am I trying to earn through planning that I could claim through action?

....

....

3. What will I do in the next 24 hours to prove "special" isn't required?

....

....

Then do it. Not because it's perfect, but because it's real.

EXCUSES ARE A FORM OF POISON. THEY PARALYZE YOU WITH FALSE REASONING AND YOU FAIL TO ACT.

—PETER LOPEZ JR.

CHAPTER 2

Excuses Are Your Poison

The Most Convincing Excuses Sound Smart. You might think fear is your greatest roadblock, but try a convincing excuse. Not the flimsy "I forgot" or "I'm too busy" type, but the high-functioning, emotionally savvy excuses wrapped in mindfulness lingo and self-preservation. These excuses are dangerous because they sound logical. They keep you stuck while making you feel clever for doing so.

"I'm not dodging it; I'm just making sure I do it right."
"It's not fear; I'm waiting for the perfect moment."
They're refined, plausible, and nearly true. Almost.

I've heard these narratives countless times, from former coaching group members, friends, colleagues, and even in my own life. The story always unfolds the same way: a deferred dream justified by a phrase that sounds like strategy.

"I'm still refining my approach."
"I'm ensuring proper alignment."
"I want to be intentional."

They appear innocuous, even admirable. But if you let them persist, they form a habitual, self-soothing cycle that keeps you revolving around your goals without ever landing. It's not failure that holds most people back, it's the excuses they've come to trust. And if you're not cautious, these excuses will sabotage your progress, slowly eroding it from the inside until all you're left with is an eloquent reason for staying put.

The True Nature of Excuses

Excuses aren't outright lies. That's what makes them so deceptive. They contain a kernel of truth, with just enough reason to shield you from discomfort. They allow you to opt out while keeping your pride intact, maintaining the façade that you're still in command. But beneath every excuse lies an unnamed, unacknowledged, and potent fear. Left unchecked, that fear doesn't merely delay action; it becomes a way of life.

I've encountered excuses dressed in ambitious language:

- "I'm still refining the concept."

- "I'm making sure it aligns with my values."

- "I want to ensure it is impactful."

These phrases don't just hinder action; they hinder your identity. They trap you in a realm where you fear rejection, error, or exposure. You're simply planning, thinking, and refining. Yet the longer you remain in that space, the more your nervous system equates hesitation with safety. You convince your brain that waiting is wise, stalling is strategic, and inaction is mature. In reality, it's just fear in an upscale disguise, costing you more than you know. Excuses don't merely stall your progress; they alter your self-perception, turning you into someone who waits instead of someone who acts.

Excuses don't keep you safe. They just keep you still.

The Enlightened Delay

Let me confess something I'm still embarrassed about: I used research as a drug. I love clarity. I crave certainty. I want to see the big picture, zoom into the details, and map every angle before I start.

When I decided to write a book years ago, I didn't just write; I researched. I devoured storytelling frameworks, studied bestsellers, and analyzed narrative arcs. I called it "deep work," "market validation," "positioning." I built Notion dashboards, bought fresh notebooks, and color-coded my notes. Every writing session turned into a brainstorm, every brainstorm into a deep dive, every deep dive into another month gone. I had the outline, the stories, the vision. I even blocked off time. But I didn't write a sentence.

I wasn't lazy; I was obsessed. I convinced myself I was doing the work because I was learning about the work. I sounded productive. Friends cheered me on when I shared my "process." I posted quotes about "trusting the journey." But four months in, I had nothing but elegant avoidance to show for it. I remember sitting at my desk one night surrounded by books and sticky notes when I opened a new tab to research "how to overcome writer's block." That's when it hit me: I wasn't blocked. I was hiding. My "research" was a ritual, a sophisticated stall tactic to avoid the mess of actually writing. I didn't lack insight; I lacked movement.

Admitting that wasn't easy, but it broke the cycle. Not dramatically, not overnight, but that honesty was the first step toward action. Not all delay is lazy. Some of it is dressed like diligence and is the hardest to spot.

I used to believe I wasn't qualified to speak on cybersecurity because I lacked the "right" credentials. Every panelist I admired held a master's or doctorate, listed an elite university on their résumé, or boasted decades at Fortune 100 firms. I told myself, "Without those qualifications, I'll mislead people." It sounded responsible, protecting my audience from half-baked advice, but it was a polished excuse masking my fear of exposure.

So, I set out to clear that hurdle. I earned two master's degrees, one in engineering and an executive master's from a top program, and stacked up industry certifications. Yet new doubts kept arising: I didn't have enough hands-on experience and no big-name client references, and I felt I still couldn't answer the toughest questions. No combination of letters after my name could quiet my inner voices.

Then, I learned about Emma Grede. She dropped out of school at sixteen, grew up as the eldest child of a single mother, and never walked the halls of an Ivy League campus. Today, she co-founded and runs two billion-dollar brands worth nearly $400 million. She didn't wait for perfect credentials. She relied on grit, vision, and relentless action.

That realization hit me like a cold splash of water. What was stopping me if a school dropout could build billion-dollar companies without an advanced degree? I began gathering my own "Emma-style" proofs. Credentials aside, I'd led major transformations, coached teams, and solved complex problems daily. I drafted a short talk, recorded it on my phone, and shared it with a trusted peer group. My heart pounded, and my inner critic offered a dozen reasons why I wasn't ready. Still, I pressed send.

The response wasn't perfect, but it was far more encouraging than the silence I feared. Colleagues thanked me for insights I'd taken for granted. One even asked if I would lead a webinar the following month.

That small victory shattered my most polished excuse. It wasn't about degrees or titles, it was about sharing my expertise.

Voices behind the excuse:

Critic: "You're not qualified; your advice is invalid without elite credentials."

Protector: "Wait until you're untouchably prepared so you don't look foolish."

Ghost: "No one will care what you say if you're not a recognized expert."

Each voice masks fear behind logical language: "I'm protecting my audience" and "I'm respecting the field."

Next, we'll strip away those "smart" excuses with the E.A.S.E. Method, exposing the fear beneath, shrinking the steps, and proving that action, not credentials, is the true gateway to credibility.

Why Excuses Feel So Safe

Excuses feel safe because they protect the future version of you, the one who's confident, prepared, and successful. If you don't act, that version stays untouched, untested, sparkling with potential. You haven't failed because you haven't tried. You haven't missed it because you haven't shot. Your ego stays intact, your dreams unblemished. But that safety comes at a brutal cost: that future you aren't growing. They're just floating above your life, imaginary and inert, while you're stuck in a cycle of "not yet."

Excuses rarely sound like "I'm scared." They sound like strategy:

- "I want it to land well, so I'll wait a bit longer."

- "I'm respecting my bandwidth."

- "I want to do it right the first time."

These phrases carry just enough logic to quiet your discomfort, but they're not about logic but fear. Specifically, the fear of what you might feel if things don't go as planned. Rejection. Uncertainty. Exposure. Failure. Excuses let you stay in the imagined version of success, where your potential remains pristine. But they cost you your evolution. The real loss isn't what you didn't do; it's who you didn't become because you never began. Every time you lean on an excuse, you choose comfort over growth; that trade-off compounds faster than you think.

The Emotional Economics of Avoidance

Procrastination isn't just a discipline problem but an emotional transaction, and the math doesn't add up. The most ambitious people delay the most because their goals matter deeply, making the stakes feel sky-high. You're not stalling because you're unmotivated; you're stalling because action might force you to face feelings you're not ready for. Let's break it down.

First, there's rejection. If you share your idea, launch your project, or apply for the role, you might learn it's not good enough, or worse, you're not. Your brain, wired to avoid social pain, treats that as a mortal threat. So, it freezes you, pushing you back to "planning" to avoid the sting. Then there's uncertainty, the foggy space between intention and outcome. Acting without knowing how it'll land is emotionally taxing, so you retreat to control, more research, clarity, and preparation, even if it's false. Imposter syndrome creeps in next: Who are you to do this?

You buffer, shrink, and edit your ambition into something safer and less exposed.

There's also the fear of public failure, not just failing but failing where people can see. The colleagues who might raise an eyebrow, the friends who might stay silent, and the strangers whose indifference feels like proof you don't belong. And then there's the quiet killer: regret for starting too late. The moment you act, you confront how long you've waited, how much time you've lost, how much you could've done if you'd started sooner. That regret is heavy, so you avoid it by staying still.

This is the emotional economics of avoidance: you buy a moment of ease and pay with your potential. The discomfort shows up: exposure, uncertainty, and vulnerability. You reach for the noble-sounding excuse, "I'm not ready." You get temporary relief, like a hit of dopamine. And then... nothing changes. You stay still. Behavioral science backs this: our brains prioritize short-term emotional safety over long-term growth, a bias called temporal discounting. But you can't build anything meaningful with that trade. The cost isn't just time but the person you're not becoming.

Let's Name It

The good news? Once you name the pattern, you're not in it anymore; you're looking at it. So, let's get honest. What's your go-to excuse? What's the version of "not now" you've made sound smart? What's your delay language, the phrase that buys you time but costs you progress? Maybe it's: "I just want to be intentional." "I need more clarity." "I'm still finding my voice." "I'm not aligned yet." "This isn't the right season."

Those aren't wrong, but if you've been repeating them for months or years without moving, they're not reasons. They're rituals, outdated survival strategies that once protected you but now hold you hostage. This isn't about attacking your fear but refusing to let it drive. Fear can come along; it just doesn't get to steer.

YOUR TWO MINUTES EXERCISE:

1. Write down your excuse, be as specific as possible.

....

....

....

2. Ask Yourself:

■ What is this protecting me from?

....

....

■ What is it costing me?

....

....

Naming it is the first step to dismantling it.

The Breakpoint: When Excuses Collapse

Excuses don't break under pressure or logic. They break under proof: evidence that the thing you feared didn't destroy you. The most powerful proof? Action. Small, shaky, imperfect, but real.

I remember a follow-up call with Priya, a student from my boot camp, after her first public LinkedIn post. She'd rewritten the caption six times, kept the tab open for three days, and nearly deleted it after posting. She was terrified of sounding "off," of being ignored or judged. But the next morning, something shifted. No trolls. No humiliation. Just a comment from a colleague: "This is exactly what I needed to hear." That single connection, one proof point, changed everything. Her excuses, so solid before, felt paper-thin. That post became a weekly habit, then a portfolio, then a side hustle. It wasn't the post that changed her; it was the proof she could act despite fear.

Another student, Alex, faced a similar wall. He wanted to pitch a new project to his team but kept delaying, saying he needed "more data" to make it airtight. The real fear? Being dismissed by his boss. I challenged him to share a rough outline in the next meeting, not a full pitch, just an idea. He did, expecting pushback. Instead, his boss asked for more details and greenlit a pilot. That small win shattered Alex's excuse that he wasn't ready. He started pitching ideas regularly once he had evidence that acting didn't end him. Proof is the antidote to excuses; it shows you the threat was never as significant as you thought.

The Subtle Shift

Here's where the game changes: you stop trying to feel your way into action and start acting your way into a new feeling. Stop asking, "Do I feel ready?" Ask, "What would a ready person do right now?" That question flips the script. You're not overcoming fear; you're bypassing it with motion. Motion, not motivation, rewires your beliefs. Confidence isn't a prerequisite but a side effect of action. Research on habit formation shows that small, consistent actions reshape neural pathways, reducing the emotional weight of fear over time. The more you move, the less power your excuses hold. You don't need to feel brave to start; you just need to begin to feel fearless.

DELAY DETOX: **START SMALL, START LOUD**

Let's detox your delay pattern right now. Don't try to overhaul your life; take one micro-move that contradicts your usual excuse. Make it small enough to feel harmless, bold enough to feel real:

■ If your reason is "I'm still refining it," publish a rough draft: a blog post, a social media update, or a sketch.

■ If it's "I'm still learning," teach what you know so far; a quick video, a comment on a forum, a note to a friend.

■ If "I'm not ready," share what you're doing while not ready; a behind-the-scenes post, an email saying, "I'm working on this."

One action, in public, with your name on it. That's the antidote. For example, if you're avoiding writing because "it's not polished," write one paragraph and share it with a friend. If you're delaying a fitness goal because "you're not in shape yet," post a photo of your first walk. If you're stalling on a career move because "you need more experience," send a message to a mentor asking for advice. Make truth louder than fear, and excuses lose their grip. The goal isn't perfection but visibility. It's proof you can act.

The Promotion She Almost Talked Herself Out Of

A few months ago, I caught up with Michelle, a former colleague who quietly held her department together. She organized chaos, coached new hires, and solved problems no one else wanted. When I asked about her next steps, she hesitated.

"I've been thinking about a leadership role," she said. "But I don't know if it's the right time." She paused, ready to justify waiting. "I want to feel more ready and fully grounded, like I can own it if challenged."

It sounded responsible, but I'd heard that line before. It wasn't about readiness; it was about permission. Michelle was already leading, mentoring, managing, and influencing. But she hadn't raised her hand. Her excuses: "I'm still finding my voice," "I don't want to overstep," "I need to learn more," hid one fear: What if I ask, and they say no? What if I'm seen as trying too hard? What if I'm exposed?

This wasn't about skills but the gap between her identity and who she was asking permission to become. I pushed her to schedule the conversation, not to pitch herself, but to share what she'd been doing and what she wanted to do more of. She did, expecting resistance. The room didn't explode. Her director listened, nodded, and offered a path forward. That small act shifted everything: not because she gained new skills, but because she stopped waiting to be chosen. She acted like someone who knew her worth. The gap wasn't timing or clarity: it was her holding herself back.

The Gap Is You

You're not waiting for clarity, alignment, or the perfect moment. You're avoiding exposure. You're not missing skills or timing; you're missing motion. You're the gap between where you are and where you want to be. You, waiting for fear to pass. You, holding your breath for certainty. You, mistaking silence for strategy. You don't need to be louder or more perfect; you need to stop being the one who keeps yourself out of the room. The voice saying "not yet" isn't wisdom; it's resistance.

And you're stronger than it.

FRAMEWORK: **FROM EXCUSE TO EVIDENCE (THE E.A.S.E. METHOD)**

When the voice in your head says, "Now's not the right time," or "Wait until you're more confident," don't argue with it; act through it. Break excuses with evidence:

1. Expose the excuse. Catch it in real time and name it plainly: "I'm telling myself I must wait until... before I act." Write it down and say it out loud.

2. Ask what it's protecting. Every excuse shields something: a fear, an identity, or a vulnerability. Ask, "If I acted today, what discomfort might I feel?"

3. Shrink the step. Make the action so small your excuse has nothing to grip. Instead of "launch a business," send one email; instead of "write a book," write one sentence.

4. Execute without editing. Take the action. Don't polish midmove. Just ship it. Doing reshapes thinking; you can't logic your way into courage.

Each small proof rewires your identity from "I wait" to "I do." You don't wait for courage; you build it, choice by choice.

Why This Works

The E.A.S.E. Method doesn't rely on motivation; it removes resistance. Excuses thrive on ambiguity, vagueness, and self-judgment, fueled by cognitive biases like loss aversion (avoiding pain over seeking gain). But when you replace that with something clear, simple, and non-negotiable, your nervous system stops seeing action as a threat. Motion breaks the cognitive loops that keep fear in charge. Behavioral science supports this: small, consistent actions create a feedback loop, reinforcing self-efficacy, the belief you can act. Each move is evidence you can face fear, and that evidence rewires your identity from "I wait" to "I do." You don't wait for courage; you build it, choice by choice.

Delay Detox: Your Exit Strategy

Here's your exit plan from the excuse cycle. When you feel the spiral starting, reset with these steps:

- **Name the delay.** Call out your go-to phrase: "I'm not ready," "I need more time," "I'm still preparing." Write it down.

- **Find the fear.** What's it protecting? Rejection? Uncertainty? Looking foolish? Be specific.

- **Pick one move.** Within the next hour, what's the smallest action you can take to prove the excuse wrong? Examples: Send a rough draft to a friend, post a 10-second story about your goal, or sign up for a class.

- **Set a timer.** Five minutes. Start. Don't edit. Just move. If you're writing, type one sentence. If you're networking, draft one message.

- **Notice the shift.** You didn't die. The world didn't end. You're still here, and now you have proof you can act.

This isn't about big wins; it's about small proofs. If you're avoiding a creative project, share one idea on social media. If you're stalling on fitness, take a five-minute walk and tell someone about it. If you're delaying a tough conversation, send a text to schedule it. Each move is a vote for the person you're becoming.

REFLECTION PROMPT: **WHERE HAVE I BEEN WAITING FOR READINESS**

Pause and write for three minutes:

■ What's the most believable excuse you've used to delay action? Be specific, e.g., "I need more clarity before I start."

_____

_____

_____

■ What fear is it protecting? Rejection, uncertainty, regret? Name it.

_____

_____

_____

■ What's one small, visible action you can take in the next 12 hours to prove that excuse wrong? A post, an email, a step?

_____

_____

_____

■ How will you feel after you do it? Lighter, stronger, freer?

Then, take that action. Not because it's perfect, but because it's yours.

The Identity Cost of Excuses

Excuses don't just delay your goals; they reshape your identity quietly and over time. Every time you retreat behind a polished rationale, your self-trust erodes like water-wearing down the stone. Every "I'll do it next month" you don't follow through on loosens your grip on your word. It's not dramatic; it's erosion, subtle but relentless. You stop trusting your timelines and believing your declarations until you stop declaring altogether. Your ideas slip into the past tense: "I was going to write a book." "I almost started a business." You begin to see yourself as someone who gets close, who knows better but doesn't do better.

Imagine your identity as a house. Every excuse is a crack in the foundation, small at first, barely noticeable. But over time, those cracks spread, weakening the structure. You start to feel like the action is pretending like you're no longer someone who follows through. This is the identity cost of excuses; not that they keep you behind schedule, but that they rewrite who you are. You think you need a better system, but you need to rebuild belief in your follow-through.

But here's the good news: it's reversible. Not with grand gestures but with tiny, gritty acts no one claps for. One small move, a sentence written, an email sent, a step taken, rebuilds the foundation, brick by brick. It's a quiet promise to yourself: "I still keep my word." That's the moment you stop needing excuses. That's when you start becoming someone who acts, not someone who waits.

VULNERABILITY
IS NOT ABOUT
WINNING, AND IT'S
NOT ABOUT LOSING.
IT'S ABOUT HAVING
THE COURAGE
TO SHOW UP AND
BE SEEN.

—BRENÉ BROWN

CHAPTER 3

When Self-Doubt Becomes A Battleground

That Inner Voice You Recognize Too Well

Self-doubt rarely announces its arrival with fanfare. Instead of blasting through with overwhelming force, it creeps in quietly, like a familiar yet unwelcome companion when you feel most inspired. You're on the verge of a breakthrough, and one idea feels vibrant and full of potential. And right then, a nagging whisper intrudes: Who are you to take this leap? In that moment, you spiral: Perhaps you haven't done enough. Maybe someone else has already nailed it. You don't have the credentials. You're not polished enough. This voice isn't vicious; it's reasoned, even gentle as if a caring but conflicted version of you is urging caution. And because it uses your language, you're tempted to trust its verdict.

I know that internal tug-of-war. Not long ago, I remember preparing for my very first board presentation as a tech consultant. I had the experience, a neatly organized deck, even a plan that made sense. Yet the night before, I was paralyzed in my living room, surrounded by scattered notes, tormented by the thought: What if I end up sounding like a fraud? What if a question catches me off guard? Who am I to lead? The voice wasn't cruel; it felt like the voice of realism draped in humility, warning me to wait until I felt "ready." I pictured the board-room, their critical eyes, my words falling flat, and I nearly surren-dered. That conflicted inner counsel, masquerading as wisdom, almost kept me in inaction. If I'd listened, I'd still be stuck in the waiting room of my potential.

Self-doubt is insidious. It doesn't merely undermine your actions; it questions your right to act. It masquerades as nobility, as if being humble and cautious were virtues, but it's a velvet cage that immobi-lizes you while offering a false sense of security. The real obstacle isn't a lack of skill but how you converse with yourself behind closed doors.

When Doubt Hides Behind Familiarity

We've all been there: overflowing with ideas, brimming with ambition, yet stalled, waiting for some inner permission slip. Self-doubt doesn't shout, "You can't." It whispers, "Not yet," sounding sensible, mature, and responsible: "I'll go once I'm ready." But that elusive "ready" rarely arrives. Doubt only retreats in the face of real, tangible progress.

We call it caution, a buffer against failure. But waiting for confidence is like waiting for perfect weather, out of your control and keeping you locked in place. Self-doubt dresses itself up as humility or strategy, but underneath is pure fear, the kind we unpacked in Chapter 2, where excuses become lethal. We cling to that familiar voice, and familiarity makes it hard to silence. When we're indifferent, it's quiet; when the stakes matter, it surfaces because daring to become new always meets resistance.

We all know the feeling. You've got ideas in spades. Your ambition is undeniable. And yet you pause, waiting for a sort of permission from that inner echo that prefers you to remain stagnant. Self-doubt never shouts outright, "You can't do this." Instead, it coaxes with "Not yet." That "not yet" can seem so sensible, mature, and responsible. You convince yourself, "I'll move when my confidence catches up." But if you're honest, that elusive day never seems to arrive. Self-doubt only retreats when confronted by tangible evidence of success.

You tell yourself it's being careful, a buffer against failure. But waiting for confidence is like waiting for the skies to clear; it's out of your control and keeps you chained to the familiar. Self-doubt dresses itself up as humility or strategy, yet underneath it all is pure fear, the very kind we dissected in Chapter 2's discussion that excuses can be lethal. You like this voice because it knows you too well, and that familiarity makes challenging it even harder. When you're indifferent, doubt doesn't whisper. But when you care and the outcome matters, doubt surfaces because you're daring to change, a new you always face friction.

The Lie: Doubt Equates to Stopping

We've been conditioned with a dangerous notion: if you doubt yourself, you're not ready. From childhood, certainty was celebrated, while questioning was seen as a flaw. Social media idolizes bold proclamations; success is framed as a smooth, unwavering march forward. Consequently, when doubt intrudes, we see it as a fatal flaw, a sign that we're inadequate. If I'm uncertain, perhaps I shouldn't be here. This belief turns every hesitant thought into a green light for retreat.

That mindset makes doubt seem noble, a shield that excuses you from risk-taking without feeling selfish. "I'm being realistic," you tell yourself, "I'm protecting myself." But realism shouldn't mean shying away. Protection shouldn't be an excuse for inertia. Confidence isn't the absence of doubt but the defiant choice to act despite it.

The Truth: Doubt Signals Growth, Not Defeat

Here's the crux of the battle: self-doubt isn't a verdict on your abilities; it's a signal that you're pushing yourself into new territory. That inner query, "Who am I to do this?" is not a mandate to stop, but a nudge that you're on the brink of something significant. Doubt doesn't refute your intelligence; it proves that you care deeply. Rainer Maria Rilke once urged us to "live the questions now." Doubt asks those questions, and it doesn't provide final answers. It invites action; it doesn't command you to retreat.

Research in psychology supports this inner conflict. The Impostor Phenomenon hits those who are genuinely accomplished; the ones who feel the chasm between their talents and ambitions. Dr. Pauline Clance's studies reveal that even high achievers wrestle with the belief that they don't belong. This cognitive dissonance, the battle between "I am capable" and "I'm not enough," is exactly what self-doubt tries to resolve. Only those who truly care about what they do will experience this ruthless inner debate; those who are too self-assured never face it. That internal clashing is the price of investing in something new.

The real challenge is not to silence the doubt but to reduce its dominion over you. You can't banish the thought, but you can choose how you react when it appears. The goal isn't to erase the voice but to diminish its influence and redirect the energy towards progress.

Everyone Battles Doubt: Even the Luminaries You Admire

Think about Maya Angelou. Despite writing countless books and inspiring millions, she confessed that every new work came with a fear of being unmasked as a fraud. If she could wrestle with self-doubt, what makes you think you're exempt? Her doubts didn't paralyze her; they spurred her forward. She transformed those inner conflicts into pages that changed lives.

Michelle Obama has also admitted to doubting her rightful place, even from the highest echelons of power. Seasoned professionals and creative thinkers often reveal, away from the public eye, moments when they questioned, "Am I really enough?" Yet what sets them apart is that they push on regardless. They've learned that waiting for an absence of doubt is a mirage; confidence is forged by the act of persevering through the turmoil.

Consider Simone, a colleague whose brilliance was undeniable. When a leadership role opened up, I assumed she'd seize it. Instead, she hesitated. "I don't think I'm ready," she confessed, measuring herself against an impossibly loud, stereotypical notion of leadership. Her inner critic had convinced her that without feeling a surge of confidence, she wasn't worthy. In the end, someone else claimed the role, someone who had silenced their doubts by sheer certainty rather than experience. Simone later admitted, with a bitter twist, that she wasn't waiting for more skills but rather for the reassuring feeling of deserving that never arrived.

Yet then there's Lena, a student in my coaching group, who trembled at the thought of applying for a cybersecurity role. "I'm not sure I know enough," she worried, afraid that success would reveal her vulnerabilities. I challenged her to view the application simply as a test run. Expecting rejection, she instead received an interview and, soon enough, an offer. Though her doubt lingered, Lena's small act began to rewrite her inner narrative, reshaping her identity from "I'm not enough" to someone who dares to show up.

I've battled that inner conflict myself. Before launching my first online course, I spent agonizing weeks perfecting every detail, convinced I wasn't an expert. I dreaded being exposed. Yet, I set a deadline and launched the course: seven days, whether I felt ready or not. The feedback wasn't overwhelming, but it was enough to quiet that nagging conflict, proving that action, not endless debate, could tip the scales in my favor.

Let Doubt Ride Shotgun

Perhaps you've tried every trick: meditation, motivational podcasts, and affirmations to silence that inner critic. But the aim shouldn't be to eradicate the voice; it should be to learn to coexist with it without letting it hijack your choices. That internal doubt can whisper warnings, but it doesn't get to control the wheel. A lack of fear doesn't define true courage; it's defined by the decision to act despite trembling knees and conflicted hearts. Acknowledge the doubt, then change the tune, and keep driving onward.

This shift forces you to reconceptualize your relationship with doubt. Instead of treating it as a definitive stop sign, see it as an uninvited passenger who gets loud right when you're on the edge of growth. You shouldn't negotiate with it or wait for its quiet departure, you must simply move forward. Every act of stepping into the unknown is a vote for yourself, gradually reshaping your identity from one built on inaction to one built on resilience.

FRAMEWORK: **THE 3 VOICES OF SELF-DOUBT**

Self-doubt isn't a monolithic critic; it's a chorus with varied voices, each fueling the inner conflict. Recognize them, name them, and counter their narrative with decisive action:

- **The Critic:** "You're not good enough." This harsh voice magnifies every shortfall, comparing you unfavorably to others. It whispers that you don't know enough that you're destined to be a fraud. Counter it with evidence, however small: a draft shared, an email sent, or a comment voiced. Let each small act drown out the critic's relentless barrage.

- **The Protector:** "You'll get hurt if you try." This softer voice, cloaked in seeming care, warns of rejection and advises inaction until conditions feel "safe." Challenge it with tiny risks, a private message here, a low-stakes application there. Such small ventures remind you that vulnerability doesn't equal defeat; it's the incubator for growth.

- **The Ghost:** "No one will care." The quietest yet most debilitating, this voice drains you with its insistence that nothing you do matters. Counter this numb nihilism by connecting; share something, even if it's small. One moment of genuine connection can shatter the ghost's hold on you.

It's not about banishing these voices by debating them into silence; it's about softly outworking them, proving with each act that you are more than your doubts.

Rewriting The Confidence Narrative

Your inner script, laden with old, conflicting messages of unworthiness from past rejections and half-praised attempts, can be rewritten. Instead of desperately trying to silence self-doubt, recast it as a signpost on your journey. Try this template: "Even though I feel [doubtful/scared/unready], I know I've [accomplished something meaningful] before. I might not feel confident right now, but I'm willing to act like someone who [takes action]. Confidence isn't a prerequisite; it's the reward of showing up." Say it aloud or write it down. With every confrontation of your inner conflict, you chip away at its grip.

Choose proof over perfection.

Anchor your growth in reality. Pick one thing you've been delaying out of fear. Don't worry if it isn't monumental; the point is to act. Let your action be visible, whether it's publishing a rough draft, sending that email you've been dreading, or daring to speak during a meeting. Each imperfect step transforms the inner dialogue from "I'm not enough" to "I have something to offer."

Building Belief One Action At A Time

Take the example of a meeting where doubt creeps in: "What if I sound foolish?" Instead of letting the question paralyze you, acknowledge the fear. Physically shift: breathe, unmute yourself, and offer a small insight. Resist the urge to over-apologize afterward; simply move on. Recognize that each brief, uncertain contribution is a building block, a brick in the foundation of your emerging self-efficacy.

And when that familiar doubt surfaces during those critical moments (the spark of an innovative idea followed by the inner question, "Who are you to do this?"), remember that the presence of this voice means you're daring to dream big. With every action, it loses a bit of its power.

Embrace The Conflict, Don't Fight It

Reflect on this: every time you act despite feeling conflicted, you weaken the hold of self-doubt. Write down what your self-doubt tends to say. Perhaps it proclaims, "I'm not experienced enough." Consider what has been lost because you've listened too closely to that inner critic: opportunities, visibility, or the chance to be heard. Then, commit to one small risk this week, even as the doubt nags. Conclude with a declaration: "Even though I feel [doubt], I'm choosing to [action] because I am someone who shows up." Committing to this micro-action proves that your capacity to act outstrips your doubts.

You don't need to be flawlessly confident to be trustworthy; you only need to stop giving self-doubt the final say. Trust in yourself builds like a muscle, a product of showing up and following through. While your fears might arise again, remember that they don't have to dictate your actions. Each time you publish that rough idea, speak that hesitant sentence, or simply show up despite uncertainty, you are reinforcing your inner strength. Confidence is not the absence of fear but the stubborn decision to move forward despite it.

WHEN DOUBT FEELS LIKE A FAMILIAR BURDEN, GROWTH IS UNCOMFORTABLE.

Why does doubt linger so persistently? Because its presence is as familiar as it is feared. If your only comfort is hesitation, then bold steps will always feel foreign, even painful. The new emotional landscape you're crafting demands that you embrace discomfort as evidence of growth. Standing at the edge of what you know may be unnerving, but breakthroughs occur precisely there.

What Lies Ahead

In Chapter 4, we tear down the barriers that stop you from actually starting. We'll explore the REAL Method: a hands-on process to turn reflection into relentless action. If you've ever found yourself saying, "I know what to do, but I just can't do it," then prepare: the next chapter is poised to shift that inner conflict into movement. For now, hold this conflicting truth close: self-doubt isn't a sign to stop; it's the very marker that you're on the cusp of growing, even if that growth comes with a clamor of inner turmoil.

Why You Should Never Feel Like You Belong

*What if your sense of not fitting in is the
key to extraordinary success?*

I found myself in a bustling conference hall, heart racing, clutching a suit that felt borrowed. Around me, polished executives mingled effortlessly, while I lingered on the outskirts, convinced I had no right to be there. Then, in the corner, I spotted someone scribbling furiously in a notebook, eyes aglow with purpose. They weren't networking; they were building.

J.K. Rowling penned the first pages of Harry Potter in Edinburgh cafés while juggling multiple jobs to get by. Dismissed from college, Steve Jobs tinkered in a garage until he reshaped technology. Neither fit the mold; and that very friction sharpened their vision, forged their resilience, and fueled their breakthroughs.

When you embrace that outsider edge instead of hiding it, you generate a force all your own. But how do you turn this paradox into consistent forward motion? That's where a deliberate system comes in.

OUTSIDERS AREN'T BROKEN.

THEY'RE UNLOCKED.

02

THE REAL METHOD

WITHOUT A SYSTEM,
CLARITY IS JUST
ANOTHER WAY TO
REMAIN STUCK.
BRILLIANT INSIGHTS
THAT ULTIMATELY
LEAD NOWHERE.

CHAPTER 4

Introducing The REAL Method

The Problem with Breakthroughs

Let me share a truth I wish I'd learned earlier: breakthroughs alone won't transform your life; systems will. You might experience a moment of sheer clarity: a cathartic therapy session, a journal entry that strikes like lightning, or a podcast that alters your perspective, only to find yourself ensnared in the same repetitive cycles just a few weeks later. It isn't about weakness or lack of commitment; it's simply that an insight without a system is like adrenaline with no outlet. Sure, your heart might race, but your feet remain firmly planted.

I learned this lesson the hard way. A few years back, I was drowning in "aha" moments. I read voraciously, devoured podcasts, and filled pages with reflections about my future, aiming to launch a creative project, pitching daring ideas at work, and rebuilding my health. I assumed I was making progress because I felt inspired, yet my reality said otherwise. One evening, I discovered a crumpled list of goals I'd written six months earlier, none of which had advanced even a little. It wasn't because I lacked motivation; I was caught in a cycle of clarity without action, and it was utterly exhausting. My intentions were bold, but my output had flatlined.

If you're reading this, chances are you've experienced the same. You're not here in search of another fleeting epiphany; you're seeking a way to ensure your clarity endures. This chapter isn't concerned with temporary highs; it's about creating a framework that turns insight into genuine progress, step by determined step.

The Insight Loop That Traps Smart People

You may find yourself trapped if you're the reflective type, always thinking before you act and insisting on doing things with care and integrity. That strength can inadvertently reveal a painful gap between what you know and what you actually do. This gap can seem like an insurmountable chasm, paralyzing you. You might mistake clarity for progress, but they aren't the same. This is the insight loop: your mind becomes ever clearer while your life remains at a standstill.

Psychology explains this phenomenon. Increased self-awareness heightens cognitive load, making you acutely conscious of your flaws and the stakes involved, which triggers analysis paralysis: where overthinking replaces action. Behavioral science refers to this as the "intention-behavior gap"; you might intend to act, but without a structure, those intentions fizzle out. In earlier chapters, we saw self-doubt creeping in with whispers of "You're not ready," and excuses taking root. The pattern remains unchanged: clarity without a system only serves to exhaust you, not to propel you forward.

You don't need more "aha" moments. You need architecture: a structured framework to bridge that persistent gap. The REAL Method provides that architecture designed to take you from being stuck to becoming unstoppable.

At my lowest point, I realized that months of performing all the "right" internal work, reading, planning, and discussing my dreams with friends, yielded nothing observable. I wasn't creating, leading, or showing up how I wanted. I learned that building a new life on mere vibes wasn't effective. Inspiration fades, and motivation is fleeting. What actually sustains change is a system, a backbone that upholds your intentions when doubt, distractions, or overthinking set in.

This isn't about summoning willpower; it's about intentional design. I needed a way to convert belief into consistent action, day after day, even when I felt like hiding. That's when I began experimenting with the framework that eventually became the REAL Method. It's neither a quick fix, a trendy hack, nor an exhortation to hustle harder. It's a straightforward structure designed to keep you moving, even when your mind protests, "Not yet." This is made for you if you've ever known what to do but struggled to do it.

Where "Motivation" Dies, Systems Begin

Let's debunk a myth: motivation isn't what you rely on. Vision boards, TED Talks, or inspiring quotes are nice, but they aren't enough. Motivation is as unpredictable as the weather, it comes and goes. What will pull you out of that downward spiral isn't a fleeting burst of enthusiasm; it's a path that carries you forward even when you don't feel like working. That's a system. As James Clear emphasizes in Atomic Habits, while goals set a direction, systems build progress. The REAL Method acts as that system, transforming your intentions into a consistent rhythm that overcomes hesitation so your dreams don't crumble under doubt or distractions.

This method isn't about chasing euphoric highs or meticulously over-planning. It's about constructing a stable framework that endures during mood dips, when self-doubt whispers, or when excuses resurface. It represents the difference between simply hoping for change and deliberately designing change, ensuring you don't merely dream but actually do.

> ## "We are what we repeatedly do. Excellence, then, is not an act, but a habit."

> **—ARISTOTLE**

THE MOMENTUM ENGINE

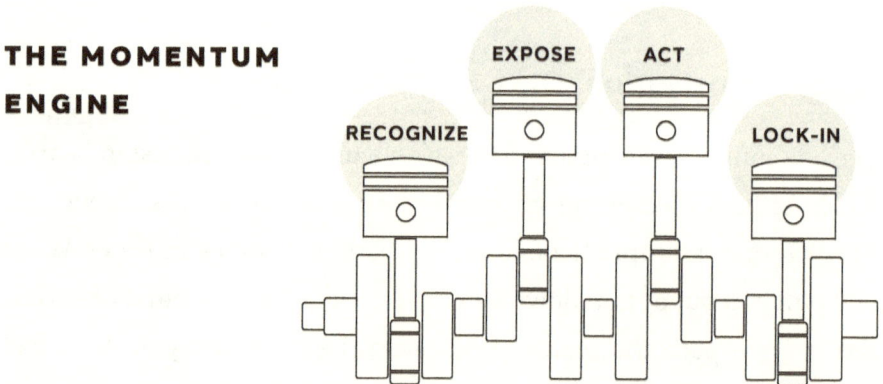

Picture your momentum like an engine. Each piston (Recognize, Expose, Act, and Lock in) fires in sequence, driving movement forward. When one misfires, the rhythm sputters. But when they're aligned, you create unstoppable motion. This isn't motivation. It's momentum you can engineer.

The Real Method: A Lifeline, Not A Theory

REAL is an acronym for four key shifts to get unstuck and stay that way. It's a lifeline based on how humans truly change rather than a lofty theoretical ideal. Here's the breakdown:

R: Recognize your patterns.

You can't alter what you refuse to acknowledge. This step involves identifying your habitual loops, be it procrastination, overthinking, or avoidance in the moment. It's not about judgment; it's about gaining clarity, much like spotting a bug in your system before it causes a crash.

E: Expose your fears.

Most of the roadblocks you encounter aren't due to laziness; they stem from unnamed fears. Naming these fears strips them of their power, turning a vague sense of dread into something tangible. This builds on earlier discussions about the three voices of self-doubt, where identifying the Critic, Protector, or Ghost diminishes their hold on you.

A: Act relentlessly.

This is about taking small, consistent steps that are visible, even if they're messy. Movement trumps hesitation every time. It isn't about waiting until you feel completely ready; it's about becoming someone who keeps moving, echoing the earlier emphasis on action over inaction.

L: Lock-in success habits.

Lasting change comes from routines you don't have to think about consciously. This step focuses on creating rituals that automatically support progress, so you never have to start from scratch each time.

Each step acts as a lever to pull you from stagnation into momentum. Together, they form a steady rhythm you can lean on when emotions falter.

It's Not A Formula. It's A Rhythm.

REAL isn't just a checklist to complete and discard; it's a dynamic rhythm you move through each time you level up. Feeling disconnected? Recognize: What's the recurring loop? Overwhelmed? Expose: What fear is holding you back? Stuck in endless preparation? Act: What is the smallest step you can take? Feeling deflated? Lock-in: What habit can you establish to automate progress? It isn't a strict rule; it's a pulse that keeps you grounded when doubt or distractions intervene.

This rhythm fundamentally reshapes your approach. Instead of chasing after motivation, you rely on a mechanism. Research in behavioral science confirms that habits formed through consistent cues and rewards rewire neural pathways, making action nearly automatic. As discussed earlier, identity shifts occur through action and not through inaction. REAL systematizes that shift, ensuring you don't just hover around your potential; you embody it.

The Founder Who Couldn't Begin

To bring REAL to life, let me share the story of Diana, a woman I encountered at a leadership summit in Austin. She wasn't the type to shout or demand attention, yet it was evident she possessed a wealth of ideas, concepts, and a quiet, intense drive. By profession, she was a cybersecurity expert garnering a rising reputation, but her real ambition was to launch her own platform: something daring, original, and truly needed. Her Notion pages were overflowing with product ideas, lists of potential startup names, and even rough wireframes drawn on the back of a children's birthday flyer. Yet none of these ideas had been brought into the light. Not even one line of code was written, no post published, and not even a soft, understated launch took place.

One night, during a reflective breakout session on the hotel rooftop, I asked her what she truly desired, not the polished version of LinkedIn. With a steady yet genuine sigh, she confessed, "I want to create something that upends the status quo, that changes how people view technology. But my mind just shuts down whenever I try to get started." I pressed further, inquiring about what she believed was hindering her progress. After a brief hesitation, she admitted, "I'm scared that if I really go for it and it doesn't work out... then I'll discover I never really had what it takes." At that moment, it was clear that her hesitation wasn't about lacking funding or skills but a struggle with her identity. The inner Critic and Ghost weren't merely whispering doubts but controlling the entire process.

A System for The Soul

Although she had never heard of REAL, we tackled it step by step. The first phase was Recognize. Diana began to notice a recurring cycle: she would get inspired, spend nights jotting down features and strategies, and then waste the following week agonizing over details like the font on a temporary landing page. Her days were filled with practical distractions: researching LLC formations, perfecting her resume, and even reorganizing her Dropbox. Yet, the actual beginning never came.

Simply charting this cycle helped her see it clearly, without judgment, only the realization of patterns.

The next phase was Expose. Diana started vocalizing her fears. "If I launch this, people might scoff, like who does she think she is?" (Ghost). "If it fails, maybe I'm not as capable as I believed." (Critic). "If I never try, at least I can claim I avoided failure." (Protector). Speaking her fears out loud diminished their grip; fear thrives in silence, but naming it makes it lose its power.

Then came Act. I advised her not to worry about launching a full-fledged company; simply make one public move. She committed to sending a single email that night outlining her product idea to a trusted contact. No pitch deck or polished copy was involved, just the raw truth. To her surprise, that email transformed into a calendar invite for a conversation. That dialog gave her the courage to launch a humble private beta signup page a week later that was unfinished and basic yet authentic.

Finally, Lock-In. Diana didn't transform overnight, but she made a vital commitment: every week, she would take at least one tangible step. Whether it was sharing a rough outline, recording a voice memo, or messaging a potential advisor, she ensured that something left her private drafts and reached the world every Friday. She even started a weekly founder diary published only to herself every Sunday with the title "What I Learned from Showing Up."

This process wasn't about building a flashy brand or scaling rapidly. It was about gaining momentum, taking action, and reclaiming her identity through consistent, visible moves.

They're Not Braver Than You: They Just Have A System

Diana's journey isn't a fairy tale with a neat ending; it's still a work in progress. But one thing is clear: those who appear to be relentlessly moving forward aren't inherently luckier or braver; they simply have systems in place to overcome fear. Incremental, visible steps triumph over the quest for perfection every time.

Others have followed a similar path. One of my students postponed applying for jobs for months until he set a rule for himself to submit one imperfect resume each day. Within a couple of weeks, interview calls started coming in. Another alum finally launched her Etsy store, not because she was fearless, but because she dedicated a 30-minute action sprint every Saturday morning.

Ultimately, it's not about eliminating fear; it's about ensuring that fear becomes irrelevant when it comes time to take action.

The Real Method as A Mirror

REAL isn't just a set of steps; it's like a mirror, reflecting at you what's happening when you feel off. Consider these everyday scenarios viewed through the lens of the three voices we discussed:

- Content creation stall: You haven't posted in weeks. Recognize that you vanish when your posts lack attention. Expose the fear whispering, "What if I'm not interesting?" (Ghost). Act by sharing one brief thought to break the pattern. Lock- in the habit by writing one draft every Friday.

- Hesitating on a job application: You keep considering applying for a challenging role. Recognize you've checked the listing several times.

Expose the thought, "If I fail, I won't be capable" (Critic). Act by submitting one imperfect resume. Lock-in a routine of applying to one role every Thursday at 10 a.m.

■ Avoiding a tough conversation: You keep delaying a difficult personal talk. Recognize that you spend far too much time drafting and redrafting your message. Expose your fear: "They might not react the way I hope" (Protector). Act by sending a short, honest message immediately. Lock-in the practice of addressing tough conversations within 48 hours.

The power of REAL isn't about achieving perfection; it's about creating momentum. This system builds upon our previous discussions about identity and action: consistently acting transforms you into someone who keeps moving forward.

Use It Backwards Too

REAL isn't solely a tool for progress; it can help you diagnose and overcome your freezes. When you feel stuck, ask yourself: Did I Recognize the pattern? Did I Expose the underlying fear? Did I Act, even in a small way? Did I Lock in a habit? If any of these steps were skipped, see it as feedback rather than failure. I remember freezing on a writing project because I was trapped in "not good enough" cycles. Looking back, I hadn't exposed the fear of irrelevance (my Ghost) or taken the small step of sharing a draft. REAL illuminated where I stalled and helped me find a way forward. It's a lifeline that always offers a way back, no matter how long you feel stuck.

The Tiny Tool That Changes Everything

Get practical now. Open your Notes app, grab your planner, or pick up your journal, and create your very own REAL Tracker:

REAL Tracker: Today's Check-In

R: What loop did I recognize today? (e.g., delaying email responses)

E: What fear or excuse emerged? (e.g., fear of coming across as unclear, Critic)

A: What micro-action did I take? (e.g., sent a brief reply)

L: What system did I adjust or create? (e.g., commit to answering one email before lunch every day)

This process takes just 90 seconds yet builds a record far more powerful than any affirmation. For instance, if you'd been avoiding a work email, you might note R: I'm delaying responses. E: I'm afraid of sounding unclear (Critic). A: I sent one reply. L: I will answer one email before lunch daily. These small wins accumulate, proving to yourself that you're capable.

Let's Build Your Real Dashboard

Take it a step further with a weekly REAL Dashboard:

REAL Dashboard: Weekly Setup

R: What's the recurring loop this week? (e.g., overanalyzing emails)

E: What's the fear driving it? (e.g., fear of sounding incompetent, Protector)

A: What's the small move I can make? (e.g., send one rough draft by Wednesday)

L: What routine can I establish? (e.g., dedicate 10 minutes each morning to drafting)

Whether you write it on a sticky note, in your journal, or use the companion worksheet, it doesn't matter how it looks; the key is to use it. As we've discussed earlier, the goal is to confront your excuses before they harden into your identity. For example, if you're stalling with your fitness goals, your dashboard could read: R: Skipping workouts. E: I'm afraid I'll look foolish at the gym (Critic). A: Walk for 10 minutes today. L: Schedule a 10-minute walk every Tuesday. These small adjustments shift your rhythm in a big way.

Your System Is Stronger Than Your Feelings

REAL isn't magical. It won't banish fear or provide endless momentum. But it does offer a reliable route back to action every time you falter. Your feelings and moods will fluctuate, and motivation will wane, but a system like REAL remains steady. It creates an external rhythm rather than relying on your internal weather. Psychological research shows that habits triggered by consistent cues and rewards become automatic, reducing your reliance on sheer willpower. This is how lasting change happens, not because you're always ready but because you've built a path that carries you even when you're not feeling it.

Consider if you're avoiding a creative project and your inner voice insists, "It's not good enough" (the Critic from Chapter 3). REAL advises: Recognize your avoidance; Expose your fear of judgment; Act by sharing one draft; and Lock in a daily writing habit. That system supports you when emotions falter, ensuring that you not only dream but also do.

This Is the Point Where Most People Quit

Often, when a system like REAL is introduced, people falter. They claim, "I'm not doing this correctly," or "I need more clarity." Sound familiar? That's the familiar voice of self-doubt, rebranded. Don't get stuck overthinking REAL; just use it. Start applying it before you feel entirely ready. Lila didn't wait for perfect certainty; her journal post was messy but real. Brandon's pitch wasn't flawless, yet it propelled him forward. The objective here isn't perfection; it's to create motion and learn through action rather than endless contemplation.

The Shift Starts Now

Stop waiting for the perfect strategy, and stop hunting for the next podcast or plan as the answer. Build a rhythm that works even when confidence or clarity is lacking because it's not about being ready; it's about moving. You're neither behind nor broken; you're in the process of building something significant. REAL is your framework for turning insight into consistent action, one relentless step at a time. As earlier lessons emphasized, action breaks the cycle of excuses and doubt. Now, REAL makes that action systematic, ensuring that you not only begin but continue to progress.

Why Real Works: The Science of Change

Let's take a closer look at why REAL is effective. It's grounded in neuroscience: habits form through repeated context-specific actions, cues spark behavior, and rewards reinforce it. REAL leverages this by prompting you to Recognize your patterns, expose your emotional triggers, Act to create action-reward loops, and finally Lock in those habits. Research, including studies by Dr. Wendy Wood, indicates that nearly 43% of daily actions are habitual, driven by systems rather than conscious decision-making. REAL turns your intentions into deliberate habits, bridging the gap between intention and action.

It also counters our cognitive biases. The status quo bias makes you cling to familiar, unproductive routines. Recognize disrupts this. Loss aversion amplifies your fear of failure, while Expose helps shrink that fear. And the endowment effect makes you overvalue planning instead of doing; until Act flips the script. By Locking in habits, you create a new default that makes progress far simpler than staying stagnant. This is not mere theory; it's essentially behavioral engineering to ensure you keep moving, even in the face of doubt or excuses.

Everyday REAL: More Scenarios to Make It Yours

To truly make REAL work for you, consider these additional scenarios, each linked to the three voices of self-doubt:

■ If you're skipping workouts due to stress, recognize that you avoid exercise when overwhelmed. Expose the fear: "I'll look foolish at the gym" (Critic). Act by taking a 10-minute walk today. Lock in the habit by scheduling that walk every Tuesday.

■ If you're blocked from writing because you edit before you begin, recognize that over-editing is holding you back. Expose the thought,

"If it's not perfect, it's worthless" (Critic). Act by writing one sentence right now. Lock in the practice of writing for at least one minute every day.

■ In a situation where you're avoiding a friend, Recognize your pattern of dodging calls. Expose the fear, "They might judge me for withdrawing" (Protector). Act by sending one brief text to check in. Lock in a routine by calling one friend weekly.

These aren't monumental gestures; they're small, consistent shifts. REAL makes these adjustments systematic, ensuring that you not only take one step but continue building an identity as someone who consistently moves forward.

REFLECTION PROMPT: **YOUR MOST BELIEVABLE EXCUSE**

Take five minutes to reflect on these three questions:

■ Where in my life do I feel most stuck right now?

....

....

....

....

....

....

....

■ Which component of REAL (Recognize, Expose, Act, or Lock-in) am I avoiding?

....

....

....

....

....

....

■ What is the smallest change I could make today to alter my rhythm?

....

....

....

....

....

....

Write down your thoughts. This moment isn't for dreaming about change; it's for making it happen. If you're stuck on a work task, for instance, note: "I'm avoiding writing a report. I skipped Expose by not naming my fear of criticism (Critic). I will draft one paragraph for my boss today." Then do it. You aren't chasing another breakthrough; you're building a lasting path.

What Happens Now?

The next four chapters will dive deeper into each letter of REAL:

■ Recognize: How to notice your recurring loops without judgment and with practical tools to break out of autopilot.

■ Expose: Techniques for naming your fears, shrinking their power, and facing them head-on.

■ Act: Strategies for building unstoppable momentum with real, visible steps, even if they're imperfect.

■ Lock-in: Methods to create lasting habits that automate your progress and keep you moving forward.

Each chapter contains exercises and mental models designed to transform how you approach challenges. Remember, you're not starting from scratch. You're building on the identity shifts from Chapter 1, the action focus of Chapter 2, and the strategies for combating doubt from Chapter 3.

FEAR RARELY
SHOUTS. INSTEAD,
IT QUIETLY
ECHOES IN YOUR
OWN VOICE.

CHAPTER 5

Your Fear Is Only a Story

The Stopping Voice

You know that moment when everything aligns, the tab is open, the camera is rolling, and the file shines with polish. You've made time for it and convinced yourself: This is it. I'm about to leap. There's a buzzing excitement inside, a spark waiting to burst into flame. Then, suddenly, a sentence sneaks in. Not from some harsh critic or random onlooker; it comes from you. Who do you think you are? This isn't enough. Someone else could do it better. Your body slows, and your fingers hover. Instead of taking the leap, you adjust a small detail, rearrange your desk, or get caught in a cycle of overthinking. That perfect moment slips away, and you find yourself back at square one.

I've been there myself. Years ago, I stood outside a meeting room, about to present a new initiative I'd spent months refining: data, vision, and slides were all lined up. As I rehearsed in my head, a soft whisper emerged: What if they see right through me? What if I'm not as ready as I believe? It wasn't dramatic or overblown; just a calm, reasonable caution, like a friend urging you to be careful. I almost backed out, convinced I needed more time to "perfect" my pitch. That voice seemed truthful then, but it was merely fear, hidden behind logic and echoing the self-doubt from earlier chapters. The clever thing about fear is its familiarity; it mimics your thoughts, and because you trust it, it keeps you stuck in a loop instead of propelling you forward.

Fear Doesn't Sound Like Fear

You might imagine fear as an overwhelming panic: a pounding heart, a sudden free-fall, that split-second before impact. Yet, the fear that governs your life is more subtle, more cunning. It doesn't scream; rather, it softly suggests with your best arguments: I must get this exactly right. I'll wait until everything is perfectly aligned. I'm simply not ready to be seen yet. It convinces you with the pretense of wisdom, strategy, and humility. But these aren't true virtues; they're just fear in disguise, keeping you motionless.

Psychology explains it this way: Fear activates the amygdala, the part of your brain that detects threats. But today's fears, rejection, failure, exposure, are not about physical danger. They're social and emotional, so your brain wraps them up in familiar narratives to make sense of them. These narratives sound reasonable, built from past experiences, doubts, and the voices of self-doubt outlined earlier: the Critic ("You're not good enough"), the Protector ("You'll get hurt"), and the Ghost ("No one will care"). You think you're hearing fear, but in reality, you're hearing caution, realism, even responsibility. Because it's in your own voice, you rarely question it. In previous chapters, we've labeled these as excuses or doubts; here, we call them stories: fear's most alluring disguise that persists because it sounds just like you.

The smarter and more invested you are, the more convincing your fear becomes. Caring more gives it better ammunition. It isn't a weakness;

it's a sign that you're truly invested. Yet, being so invested while avoiding exposure traps you in a cycle that only you have the power to break.

"The cave you fear to enter holds the treasure you seek."

— JOSEPH CAMPBELL

The Stories We Tell Ourselves

The real enemy isn't failure but the narrative you weave about what failure means. You aren't truly afraid of sharing a post that goes unread; you're worried that silence translates to insignificance. You don't fear a job rejection; you fear it as proof that you aren't qualified. You're not reluctant to start something messy; you're terrified that the mess will reveal you aren't enough. Neuroscientist Dr. Lisa Feldman Barrett sums it up: "The brain isn't only avoiding danger; it's avoiding the death of your identity." Fear isn't about keeping you safe physically; it's about protecting your self-image by avoiding actions that challenge who you believe you are.

This is exactly why delays happen. Delays feel noble: you think you are being deliberate, protecting your inner peace, or seeking clarity. But let's be honest; you're not waiting for clarity; you're dodging vulnerability. Previously, we warned against waiting for that magical moment of perfect readiness. We showed how excuses hide fear and how doubt signals caution. Now, we dive deeper: your fear is a story woven from memories, assumptions, and old wounds. It keeps you safe by keeping you small. You've clung to this narrative for so long that it seems like fact, but you have the power to rewrite it through exposure.

What They Don't Tell You About Fear

Here's an unspoken truth: the more thoughtful you are, the more persuasive your fear becomes. The higher your standards, the more refined your reasons for staying small. Fear doesn't diminish with intelligence; in fact, it sharpens. The most visionary people I've coached, with the boldest dreams, often have the smoothest excuses. They won't call it fear; they'll call it planning, preparation, or protecting their energy. Yet, those words become shackles that keep you in place over time.

Cognitive psychology explains why. These thoughts form strong neural pathways when unchallenged, making these fear stories feel increasingly valid each time you repeat them. Cognitive dissonance adds weight: when your actions (or lack thereof) conflict with your goals, your brain rationalizes the delay to ease the discomfort, reinforcing the narrative. The tragedy is that the more you care, the greater the risk of staying stuck because your fear sounds so rational. It isn't laziness; it's a narrative loop that breaks only when you confront it head-on, as we've started discussing with the REAL Method in the previous chapter.

Real Fear Vs. Story Fear

Let's make a clear distinction:

Real fear is instinctive and tied to survival. It's the jolt you feel when a car swerves near you, the impulse to run from imminent danger. It's immediate, physical, and ultimately useful.

On the other hand, story fear is constructed: a narrative spun from memories, assumptions, and emotional wounds. It's the dread of judgment, rejection, or even silence. It feels real because it borrows your logic, but its purpose isn't to protect you; it's to hold you back.

Story fear is essentially an emotional coping loop designed to skirt discomfort rather than real danger. You're not really scared of showing a draft of your work; you're terrified of what the silence might imply about your worth. Recognizing this distinction is crucial. While real fear can save you from immediate harm, story fear keeps you trapped. Recall the three voices we've identified: the Critic, the Protector, and the Ghost; they are manifestations of story fear, not objective truths. Confronting and exposing them, as discussed with the Expose rhythm in the previous chapter, is the key to breaking their hold.

REFLECTION PROMPT: **YOUR FAVORITE COMFORTING LIE**

Write down the fear that is holding you back. Ask yourself:

- What is the worst that could happen if this fear came true?

....

....

....

■ Which part of me is trying to stay safe?

....

....

....

■ When did I first learn that failure was unacceptable?

....

....

....

This isn't about blaming your past; it's about reclaiming control of your story.

A Turning Point in My Perspective

During the pandemic, I became part of a private coaching group: a small, carefully chosen circle of women who were either building, transitioning, or trying to figure things out. It wasn't glamorous; it was just Zoom meetings, voice notes, and Google Docs filled with unfinished thoughts and late-night ideas. That's when I met Samara. Quiet and thoughtful, she was the kind of person who would say just a couple of sentences and leave you reflecting on them for hours.

Samara kept journals brimming with insights: raw reflections, training outlines, and voice memos recorded after breakthroughs with clients. Despite spending years helping others move forward, her own ideas had never seen the light of day. She hadn't made any public posts, launched programs, or shared any offers. Not because she wasn't capable but because she was afraid.

"I know I'm good," she admitted in one of our breakout sessions. "But I'm terrified that if I share this and no one reacts, I'll finally have proof that it's all just in my head."

That declaration hit me like a mirror reflecting my fears. I've felt that too: the dread that if you put yourself out there, the silence might validate your deepest doubt: that you aren't as impactful as you believe.

Her fear wasn't about the quality of her work; it was about who she was. Instead of concealing her work, she was hiding herself because facing rejection of her identity felt unendurable.

Months later, she messaged me: "Remember that coaching idea I mentioned? I finally sent it to three people." One person replied, eventually booking a session that turned into a testimonial. That testimonial gave her enough confidence to share her idea publicly. It wasn't a viral hit or a flawless launch. It was real. Her next message read, "I still feel fear. But I don't believe everything it tells me anymore."

That's the pivotal moment, not when fear vanishes, but when it no longer holds the power to stop you.

The Client Who Stayed Frozen

Consider another example. I once coached a woman we'll call Jasmine. Mid-career, highly skilled, she wanted to move into more meaningful work. For nearly a year, she talked about launching a new service. Every time we spoke, she had a fresh idea, a new logo, or a better name, but the launch never happened.

I eventually asked her to pinpoint exactly what she was afraid of. After a pause, she said, "If I put this out there and it doesn't work, I'll feel stupid, like everything I built was for nothing."

This wasn't about laziness; it was fear disguised as cautious reasoning.

We then went through an early version of what I now call the Fear Audit. She discovered that her fear wasn't about failing but losing her identity as "the competent one." Her inner Critic whispered, "You're supposed to be further by now," while her inner Protector urged her to stay in the comfort zone where she was already respected, avoiding the risk of starting small.

But we broke it down. She made one small request: just one tiny action. Not a full pitch, merely a brief message to someone she trusted. That small step debunked the illusion that her fear was guarding her. Instead, it was merely holding her hostage.

How To Deconstruct a Fear Narrative

Here's a method to dismantle the story fear constructs:

1. Identify the Pattern

Determine precisely what you're avoiding. For example: "I'm scared that if I share this new idea and no one responds, I'll end up feeling invisible." This isn't just a general fear but a specific haunt from past doubts. Or "If I apply and get rejected, I'll appear as if I overreached," which echoes the voice of that internal critic.

2. Trace Its Origins

Reflect on when this fear first took hold. Perhaps it began when you were spoken over in a meeting, or when a parent warned you not to embarrass yourself, or from a time you bared your soul only to be met with silence. You don't need to rehash your entire history; just trace the narrative back to its roots.

3. Question the Evidence

Ask yourself, "If the worst happens, what would it really mean about me?" Chances are, nothing permanent will occur. More often than not, the result is simply discomfort, not devastation. Fear exaggerates, turning a negative response into an irreversible verdict, but it isn't.

4. Rewrite the Story

When fear says, "This has to succeed, or I'm a fraud," counter with, "Even if it doesn't work out, I'm someone who learns, adjusts, and tries again."

NOW, TRY THIS

Choose one fear that's been steering your decisions.

- Ask yourself:

- What am I truly afraid of?

- What story is this fear talking about who I am?

- What would I do if I believed I could handle the outcome?

Then jot this down: "I can endure the discomfort. I can't grow if I don't act." Read it every morning before you even pick up your phone.

Your New Script

The aim isn't to be fearless, that's a myth. The goal is to stop letting fear have editorial control over your life.

HERE'S A SCRIPT THAT HAS HELPED ME:

"I may not feel ready, but I'm still moving forward. I might fear being misunderstood, yet I'm showing up anyway. I don't need to silence the fear; I just need to stop obeying it."

And here's one from Samara, months after her first real offer went live: "Fear still shows up, but now it rides in the passenger seat. I'm the one driving."

FEAR AUDIT: **A 5-MINUTE RESET**

Take a moment to answer these:

- What am I avoiding right now?

- What fear lies behind this avoidance?

- When have I felt this before?

- What is this fear trying to protect me from: shame, judgment, or failure?

- What's really likely to happen if I act? What's the new story I can tell?

Consider these examples:

Posting a New Idea

■ Avoidance: Not sharing it publicly.

■ Fear: "No one will care" (an echo of past doubts).

■ Past: A time you shared something important and received no response.

■ Protection: A fear of being invisible.

■ New Narrative: "I create to connect, not to prove."

Asking for Help

■ Avoidance: Reaching out.

■ Fear: "They'll think I'm incompetent" (the critical voice within).

■ Past: A moment in school when a question was mocked.

■ Protection: Holding onto self-worth.

■ New Narrative: "Asking for help is a strength, not a weakness."

Having a Difficult Conversation

■ Avoidance: Confronting a friend.

■ Fear: "It'll only make things worse" (the protective instinct).

■ Past: A friendship that deteriorated because conflict was avoided.

■ Protection: Guarding emotional safety.

■ New Narrative: "I value truth, and I can manage the discomfort."

What Most People Do Wrong

Many wait for fear to disappear completely, or, even worse, they avoid any situation that triggers fear. But fear isn't a stop sign; it indicates that you're close to something meaningful. Shunning fear might feel safe, but it only keeps you from growing.

A Personal Moment

This book nearly never existed; not because I doubted its worth, but because I cared too deeply about its outcome. I understood its significance and was terrified it might fall flat with a thud of silence. So, I kept "working on it," researching, tweaking, and reading others' books more than writing my own.

Then I asked myself: What's scarier? Publishing it and facing potential silence or never publishing it and haunting myself with that silence forever?

From that day forward, I committed to writing 100 words every day. Some days, I erased them; other days, they blossomed into five pages. But I kept moving forward, and every line became evidence that fear doesn't get to decide my path.

YOUR TURN

Take a moment now to write down:

■ The fear that has been dominating your inner dialogue.

....

....

....

■ The narrative it creates about who you are.

....

....

....

■ The alternative truth you want to believe instead.

....

....

....

Underline this: "This fear is loud, but it is not my truth."

Coming Next: Chapter 6 – Act Now, Confidence Later

We're done waiting. In the next chapter, we take deliberate action, not because we feel completely ready but because readiness follows action. We'll explore how to take small yet bold steps that shape our identity rather than overthinking or striving for perfection. Let's move forward together.

"

CONFIDENCE IS A REWARD, NOT A REQUIREMENT.

"

Act Now, Confidence Later

The Confidence Trap

For years, I believed a lie that kept me stuck, I thought that once I felt confident, I'd be ready to start. It sounded logical, even wise, to wait for that perfect moment when I'd wake up feeling certain, with calm nerves, to speak, post, or pitch an idea. I endlessly refined drafts, scrolled for inspiration, and reassured myself I was "almost there." Sound familiar? That misconception has immobilized more people than fear ever has.

Confidence doesn't precede action; it's the reward you earn for showing up despite your fears. It isn't the starting line, but the consequence of moving forward. Waiting for it becomes a trap that keeps you going in circles instead of taking action. Just as Chapter 1 warned against waiting for an elusive spark, Chapter 3 revealed that hesitation only fuels doubt, and Chapter 5 taught that fear is just a story you tell yourself. This chapter shatters the myth that you need to feel confident before acting. The key is to move first and let confidence catch up along the way.

When you idolize confidence, you let your decisions depend on feelings instead of actions. You treat confidence like the ultimate permission slip. No confidence? No action. Instead, you end up scrolling, organizing, or "calibrating," always convinced that you're on the edge of being ready. But how many weeks have slipped away under the guise of being "almost there"? How many brilliant ideas have been buried by endless waiting?

I once called this standby phase "preparing," waiting for the perfect headspace to launch a project. As my notes piled up, progress stalled, and that headspace shrank with each delay. Waiting creates a vicious cycle: no action, no progress, and no evidence of success. Behavioral psychology's intention-behavior gap shows that without structure, good intentions wither. While Chapter 2 explained how excuses widen this gap, and Chapter 4 introduced the REAL Method to bridge it, this chapter teaches that action, not a perfect mindset, breaks the loop. Confidence is the result of moving, not the cause.

Self-perception theory, developed by Dr. Daryl Bem, reveals that we don't act because we already believe, rather, our actions shape our beliefs. When you take action, your brain observes your behavior and builds your identity. Posting daily makes you a creator, facing rejection builds resilience, and launching an imperfect idea shows you're a risk-taker. Each act is like a vote for the person you want to become, echoing the Identity Spiral from Chapter 1.

Neuropsychology supports this idea. Taking action forges neural pathways that reinforce behaviors. Dr. Carol Dweck's research on the growth mindset shows that effort, rather than innate talent, forms self-belief. Dr. Albert Bandura's self-efficacy theory further explains that even small mastery experiences build confidence. Every action signals, "I'm capable." And as Dr. B.J. Fogg's behavior model points out, the dopamine released from these small wins cements the habit. In contrast, waiting only leaves you stuck, while Chapter 3's three voices, the Critic, the Protector, and the Ghost, gain strength. Movement quiets them and builds confidence naturally.

> "You gain strength, courage, and confidence by every experience in which you really stop to look fear in the face."
>
> — **ELEANOR ROOSEVELT**

My Favorite Lie

I used to tell myself that I couldn't go public until I felt completely "clear." I convinced myself I was "protecting my voice," avoiding "brand confusion," and polishing my message before sharing it consistently. It seemed noble, but in reality, I was waiting until I felt like the person who already had it all together before stepping into the light. I watched others post, speak, and lead, all while believing my ideas were some-how more profound. Meanwhile, no one saw them. I wasn't building anything; I was clinging to an ideal of waking up confident and visible.

Then, one day, fed up with the delay, I posted a two-paragraph reflection from my Notes app, scribbled in line at a coffee shop. It wasn't a masterpiece, just raw and honest. Someone commented, "This is exactly what I needed." It wasn't perfect, but it was real. That moment sparked a shift in me. I began chasing consistency over clarity. I started recording every post in a notebook with notes like, "Shared today, felt shaky, but proved I'm visible." The fear of appearing unprepared gradually faded, replaced by undeniable evidence that I was enough. As Chapter 4's Act step demonstrated, taking action triumphs over hesitation, and Chapter 5's Fear Audit showed that naming your fear (like the Ghost whispering "No one cares") only diminishes its power. My experience proved that action builds confidence.

Here's a truth no coach will sugarcoat: your first steps will feel cringeworthy. You're supposed to cringe at your early work, not because it's bad, but because you took action without evidence of perfection. That little moment of discomfort is a sign of bravery. True confidence isn't about dodging cringe but moving forward despite it. Holding onto a "perfect or nothing" mindset doesn't safeguard your brand; it stifles growth. In fact, the only people who never cringe at early work are those who never began in the first place.

Consider the creators you admire. Their very first post or project was likely rough and unpolished. They didn't wait for perfection; they acted, and their confidence grew later. Chapter 5's Samara emailed a raw, unedited pitch, and Chapter 4's Jasmine shared an unrefined idea. For them, visibility, not flawlessness, drove progress. If you're hesitating to share because you feel it's "not ready," you're hiding instead of evolving. Embrace the cringe, be visible, and allow growth to blossom in the mess.

QUICK EXERCISE: **YOUR CRINGE INVENTORY**

■ Identify one post, video, or project you've held back because it wasn't "ready."

....

....

■ Reflect on the story you tell yourself about sharing it (for example, "It'll flop").

....

....

Flip it:

■ What might happen if you share it just as it is?

....

....

....

....

■ What if this act of visibility is the missing piece for your growth?

....

....

....

....

Micro-Proof: The Secret to Believability

Confidence isn't the result of one grand success; it's built up from tiny bits of evidence that you take action. Think of it as a mental highlight reel: write 200 words, and you've shown your writing ability; share a thought, and your voice matters; say no to a bad deal, and you reinforce your self-worth. Every small action is a receipt of progress and identity. The more receipts you gather, the less power Chapter 3's critical voices have over you.

When your mind insists that you're not ready, these micro-wins say, "I started." Behavioral science confirms that small victories trigger dopamine, reinforcing behavior and building self-efficacy. While Chapter 4's REAL Tracker logged actions, micro-proof captures shifts in identity. It isn't about feeling confident from the start; it's about accumulating evidence that you are capable of making doubts disappear. Whether it's Amira's candid email or my coffee shop note, every act is a piece of proof. Start collecting yours.

ACTION PROMPT: **THE CONFIDENCE LOOP**

Let's get tactical with a three-step framework, the Confidence Loop, that breaks the cycle of overthinking and builds self-belief through action. Use it when you catch yourself waiting for the perfect moment.

Step 1: Start Before You're Ready

Pick a step so small it almost feels ridiculous. Instead of preparing a full proposal, send a quick message. Rather than writing a complete book, jot down one paragraph. Instead of changing your life overnight, take one action that aligns with your goal. This tiny step bypasses your brain's demand for certainty, embedding movement in your nervous system. This mirrors Chapter 2's E.A.S.E. Method, where small actions dismantle chains of excuse.

Step 2: Capture the Micro-Proof

Right after you act, take about 60 seconds to note down:

- What you did

- How it felt

- What it proves about you

For example: "Sent a rough email pitch. It was scary but freeing. This shows I'm proactive." This practice cements the experience into your identity. Without it, your actions remain unrecognized, and your confidence weakens.

Step 3: Repeat and Reflect

Repeat this loop until it becomes a habit. Every repetition teaches your nervous system that this isn't danger but growth. Reflect on your progress weekly: What receipts have you collected? This loop functions like Chapter 4's REAL rhythm, gradually making action your default. Over time, confidence becomes second nature.

Visualize a circular diagram with arrows moving from "Small Action" to "Micro-Proof Capture" to "Ritual Repetition," all summing up in the label "Confidence Loop: Identity Built by Evidence."

Example Loop:

- Action: Post a one-sentence update on LinkedIn.

- Micro-Proof: "I shared despite fear. I felt awkward, but it proves I'm visible."

- Repeat: Post daily for a week while logging each experience.

What You Think You Need vs. What You Actually Need

Many believe they require:

- Complete clarity on every step.

- A stack of skills or certifications.

- A flawless plan.

- A mentor's validation.

In truth, what you really need is:

- Momentum built from small steps.

- Visibility, even if it's imperfect.

- Tangible proof of progress.

- Comfort with discomfort.

- A willingness to embrace messy action.

Courses, tutorials, or systems can help, but without action, they're just background noise. The journey from knowing what to do to becoming who you want is paved by action. Chapter 1's Identity Spiral showed that you evolve by doing, and Chapter 5's Fear Audit demonstrated how naming your fears helps you overcome them. Action transforms your potential into reality.

Pick that idea, draft, or pitch you've been perfecting in secrecy, and share it as it is. Don't seek approval, feedback, or a new template. Just put it out there, even if it's rough. "Ugly" is simply the starting line for progress. Your breakthrough might look like something you are initially reluctant to show, but don't let your ego stop you, allow movement to lead.

The Real Confidence Builders

Who truly becomes confident? Not the loudest, not the most polished, nor those waiting for absolute certainty, but the people who act even when they're not sure. Consider these examples:

The Manager Who Didn't Wait for a Title

Selene, whom I met through a coaching cohort, worked in operations without a title or formal promotion. But she started leading projects, mentoring juniors, and owning deliverables. Eventually, she told her manager, "I've already been doing the job. I'd like the role to reflect that." She got the promotion because she acted before she felt fully 'qualified.'

The Teen with the Blog

Malik, a high school student obsessed with tech, started a blog explaining what he was learning. His grammar was rough, and his site was clunky, but the consistency built confidence. An educator shared one post, and within a few months, he had people reaching out to collaborate. His identity shifted from "just a kid learning" to "someone who teaches what he knows."

The Artist Who Shared Her Sketches

Clara had dozens of sketchbooks stacked in her closet. One day, she snapped a photo of a drawing she didn't even like that much and posted it. To her surprise, people resonated with it. That single step led to more posts and a pop-up market invite. Confidence wasn't born from hiding; it was built through sharing.

These aren't unicorns. Chapter 4's Jasmine and Chapter 5's Samara did the same. Confidence is the consequence of courageous action.

The Identity Shift

Confidence isn't simply a feeling; it's the byproduct of self-trust built on evidence of your own actions. This self-trust arises when each action reinforces who you say you are. The shift in mindset is: I'm not waiting to feel confident; I'm becoming confident every time I move through fear. The real you isn't hidden behind another course or journal entry; it's waiting just on the other side of your next imperfect step.

THE MOMENTUM LADDER

When doubt begins to spiral, use the Momentum Ladder to shift from paralysis to action by stacking small, consistent steps.

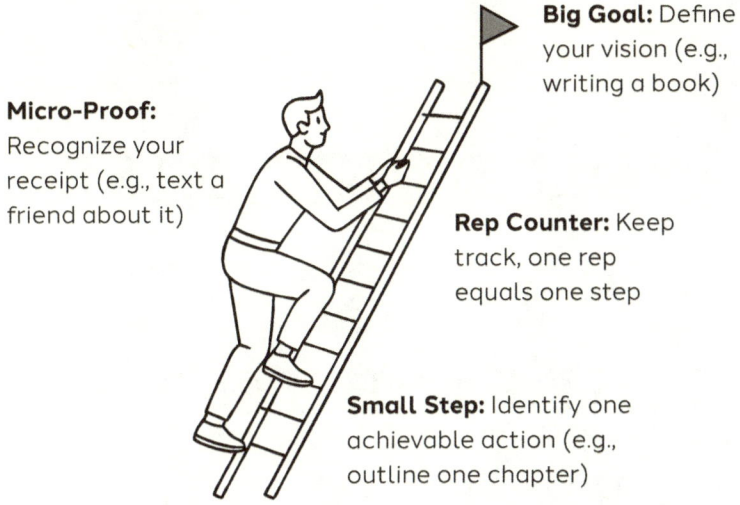

Big Goal: Define your vision (e.g., writing a book)

Micro-Proof: Recognize your receipt (e.g., text a friend about it)

Rep Counter: Keep track, one rep equals one step

Small Step: Identify one achievable action (e.g., outline one chapter)

Each rung moves you forward. No motivation required, just proof.

"

YOU DON'T RISE TO YOUR GOALS. YOU FALL TO THE LEVEL OF YOUR HABITS.

"

CHAPTER 7

Habits Are Everything

For the longest time, I believed that the size of my goals defined my potential. Big, bold ambitions were supposed to scare me into action. If my dreams didn't unsettle me, then I clearly wasn't aiming high enough. We're often told to dream big, reach for the moon, and never settle. So, I set out to create audacious goals. I spent countless hours putting together a vision board filled with my ideal future: business targets, personal milestones, transformations in health and fitness. In those early days, I felt empowered by the grand vision taped to my wall, a shining reminder of what could be. For a short stretch, a few days or maybe even a week, I rode that surge of motivation, feeling unstoppable.

But soon enough, that excitement would fade, leaving only a glossy reminder of a life I wasn't living. I'd gaze at those lofty targets and feel disappointment and confusion. How could something so clear and inspiring become meaningless just days later?

After cycling through these highs and lows for years, I finally grasped a hard truth: goals alone won't get you far. Life doesn't advance toward what you want; it shifts toward what you consistently do. You don't rise to your ambitions. Instead, you settle into your habits.

I began to see my life as a tapestry of routines, small actions that slipped by unnoticed but which, over time, set the course for my future. There were morning rituals that I practiced without a second thought, automatic responses to stress, and end-of-day behaviors that had become predictable. They all might seem mundane, even boring, but these seemingly trivial routines were far more influential than any goal-setting session ever was.

The gap between my vivid vision and daily reality was the real problem, not a lack of ambition. Goals pointed me in the right direction, yet my everyday habits determined where I actually ended up. Unfortunately, my routines were not in alignment with the life I promised myself.

"Continuous effort — not strength or intelligence — is the key to unlocking our potential."

— WINSTON CHURCHILL

I remember the moment I truly understood this. It was a Tuesday evening. I had just dropped another ambitious project midway and was disheartened. I closed my laptop and reached for my phone out of habit, ready to immerse myself in endless scrolling—a repeated behavior I'd fallen into without even thinking about it. But then something unexpected happened. In that pause, I became aware of the automatic response, and clarity set in: my outcomes were not reflections of my grand ambitions; they were the result of countless tiny choices made day after day.

I soon noticed my habits everywhere: the instant reach for sugar when stressed, dodging difficult conversations until resentment built up, and choosing distractions over the deep work I knew mattered most. Each small decision might seem trivial, but together, they painted the stark picture of why my big goals always seemed out of reach.

Here's the key point: whether or not you feel disciplined, you already have a system in place. Routines govern your days, even routines you never consciously chose. Your brain craves consistency and predictability, which is why it locks you into repeated behaviors, even if those behaviors contradict your biggest aspirations.

Realizing that was both liberating and intimidating. It meant that if habits create your reality, then you have the power to reshape it. It also meant facing the thousands of small, automatic decisions that fill your day and deciding to change them.

I knew that if I wanted a different life, I needed to rewrite those invisible scripts.

That transformation, from chasing grand dreams to refining daily disciplines, didn't happen overnight. It took small, deliberate experiments. I started with something that seemed insignificant at first. Rather than setting a goal to write a book, I decided to write for just five minutes each morning. Instead of vowing to completely overhaul my fitness, I committed to ten minutes of movement every day.

At first, these changes felt trivial. Ten minutes of movement wasn't life-altering. But over time, those small daily actions began to add up. They were not intimidating, so I did them consistently. And with every modest commitment kept, my self-image started to shift.

Gradually, a deeper change took hold, one more powerful than fleeting motivation. It was the shift in identity. I was evolving into someone who kept their word daily, not merely when I felt inspired. Each tiny action wasn't just another task checked off but a vote cast for the person I wanted to become, someone who no longer waited for motivation to strike but relied on steady routines that built resilience.

Consider this reflection: one habit you perform without thinking, such as scrolling on your phone, casts a vote for an identity that maybe celebrates distraction. Flip it around: What simple habit could instead vote for a more focused, intentional identity? Remember, your habits are your votes.

Habits aren't glamorous. They don't promise instant transformations or viral success. They don't lend themselves to flashy social media posts or motivational videos. From the outside, they might look mundane. Yet, it's precisely that quiet consistency that wields real power. Habits don't demand grand gestures; they thrive on the repeated, uncelebrated actions performed every day, slowly but surely building your identity.

As my small habits accumulated, they generated unstoppable momentum. Writing a few lines every morning built into chapters; chapters turned into drafts, and drafts eventually became finished works. Ten minutes of daily movement evolved into regular workouts that reshaped my body and confidence.

The most significant transformation, however, was internal. Each repeated small action bolstered my trust in myself. My confidence no longer rested on one big win but on a steady track record of consistently fulfilling small promises.

You've likely experienced this process without realizing it, whether learning to drive, mastering a new recipe, honing an instrument, or acquiring a new language. Proficiency wasn't achieved from a single moment of brilliance; it was built over time through quiet, relentless practice. It wasn't raw motivation or ambition that propelled you forward; it was repetition.

Scientific research helps us understand why habits are so effective. They form in the basal ganglia, automating repeated actions to save energy, as experts like Dr. Charles Duhigg noted. Each repetition reinforces neural pathways, much like Dr. Norman Doidge's work on brain plasticity shows. And dopamine, released by small wins, encourages you to maintain the loop, as Dr. B.J. Fogg's behavior model explains. Unlike motivation, which can vanish under stress, habits become your brain's default mode. They build identity just as the Confidence Loop in previous chapters built self-belief. The internal voices: the Critic ("You're not disciplined"), the Protector ("Don't overdo it"), and that lingering Ghost ("It's pointless"), gradually lose power when action becomes automatic. Repetition, not raw talent, makes lasting change inevitable.

So why do so many of us ignore this simple truth when we strive for major changes? It's because we're dazzled by highlight reels. We see other people's finished novels, thriving businesses, sculpted bodies, and successful relationships, which all seem to have appeared overnight. Yet we miss the countless quiet mornings spent faced with blank pages, years of building trust quietly, and unnoticed efforts that go into every visible win.

Consider someone you admire: a novelist, a leader, or an athlete. Now imagine the early mornings when they rose before dawn, faced their blank page or training session with determination, and steadily chose discipline over comfort. That's the true highlight reel: unremarkable, everyday rituals that compound over time. These are the habits that define who you become.

When I finally embraced this perspective, I stopped measuring success only by the big wins. I began to value the invisible victories: the small, private moments of consistency that no one else celebrated but that built something real and enduring. It wasn't dramatic, but it was authentic. And precisely this reliable repetition, not a burst of ambition, propelled my life forward.

Instead of waiting for inspiration, I learned to create a structure where small, intentional routines pave the way to lasting outcomes. Ask yourself not "What grand goal can I achieve?" but "Who do I need to become today to ensure tomorrow's success?"

The answer is usually straightforward and practical: someone who shows up consistently in small ways every day.

Over the coming pages, I'll share strategies for building these habits, not by relying solely on willpower or endless discipline, but by fine-tuning your environment, cues, and daily routines. You'll see how to choose habits that truly matter, make them nearly effortless, and sustain them even when motivation wanes.

Before diving into the tactics, remember this pivotal idea: your habits aren't merely part of your life; they define it. Goals map out your direction, but habits lay the road you travel. Without strong habits, even the most compelling destination becomes out of reach.

It's time to stop searching for elusive bursts of inspiration and start constructing the everyday structure that makes your future inevitable.

Highlight Reel vs. Real Life

It's tempting to compare your beginning to someone else's polished result. We idolize the success we see, such as finished novels, thriving careers, perfect bodies, and flourishing relationships. But those are highlight reels, not the full story. The backstage is filled with unnoticed rituals, small sacrifices, and everyday habits that nobody celebrates.

Social media often distorts this reality, making us believe that results should appear quickly and with minimal effort. Our gradual progress can feel discouraging when we compare ourselves to these curated images. Yet, consider for a moment the quiet routine behind every admired achievement: the early rising, the solitary work, the commitment to daily progress even when no one is watching. This is the real story of transformation.

When I embraced this understanding, my perspective shifted. I stopped obsessing over visible milestones and began to honor the daily, invisible wins, the discreet decisions that, over time, built a robust and lasting change. It wasn't glamorous, but it was genuine. And it proved that a consistent routine is the true engine of growth.

Becoming on Purpose

Many people mistakenly see habit-building as an exercise in managing discipline, sacrificing pleasure today for a distant reward. But habits are less about rigid sacrifice and more about forming an identity, defining who you are. Every small action casts a vote for the person you wish to become. If you write a little daily, you're voting for yourself as a writer. If you hit the gym even briefly, you affirm your commitment to health. And if you speak up when it feels challenging, you're shaping yourself as someone brave and authentic.

This is the beauty of habits: they're not just behaviors. They're declarations of identity. Each small, repeated action whispers to your subconscious, "This is who I am." Change doesn't happen overnight; it happens gradually as each tiny vote builds up to form a new identity. When you write every day, each paragraph is a small rebellion against the voices that doubt you. Habits align your actions with your aspirations, making fear and doubt disappear.

Ask yourself: Who do you want to become? Not "What do I want to achieve?" but "What identity do I want to embody?" When you build habits around an identity, discipline transforms from a burdensome sacrifice into an expression of who you truly are.

Remember:
My habits are my identity.

The Invisible Wins That Matter Most

There is quiet heroism in the everyday choices that go unseen: the small decisions you make when no one is watching. We often celebrate dramatic accomplishments, like a big promotion or a published work.

Still, the true engine of progress lies in the unnoticed moments: studying a bit each night, making a difficult phone call, or simply showing up on days when you feel like quitting. These wins matter most, even though they rarely receive applause.

When we overlook these tiny victories, we miss the real transformation process. Change is not a single leap; it's a marathon of consistent, uncelebrated steps. Every habit is an investment in the person you're becoming, and much like compound interest, these small, repeated actions grow exponentially over time.

Once I stopped seeking visible validation and honored my invisible consistency, my life changed in subtle yet powerful ways. It wasn't flashy or dramatic; it was reliable, day in and day out. I wasn't chasing sporadic bursts of motivation but creating momentum built on unwavering, daily habits.

From Vision to Ritual

Transforming your life isn't about chasing lofty visions alone; it's about developing humble, manageable rituals. Goals are inspiring and provide direction, but the daily rituals construct the bridge to your future. Without those rituals, even the most compelling vision remains just a dream.

The secret is to break down your aspirations into simple, repeatable actions. You don't start by running a marathon. You begin by lacing up your shoes each morning. You don't launch a business overnight; you begin by making one phone call, email, and conversation at a time. While goals face the future, rituals anchor you in today's reality.

I discovered this truth when I committed to writing daily. The grand goal of publishing a book was intimidating, but the ritual of simply opening a document and writing one sentence each day was completely manageable. Over time, that one sentence turned into pages, pages formed chapters, and eventually, those chapters became the finished work you see today. The ritual created the outcome, not the goal itself.

You can apply this approach to any ambition. Transform your grand visions into daily, actionable rituals. If you want to be healthier, start by preparing one nutritious breakfast. If you aspire to be a confident speaker, begin by sharing one thought each week. Ritualize your dreams into a routine, and watch as consistency makes them inevitable.

THE HABIT ANCHOR FRAMEWORK

CUE	ACTION	REWARD	TRACK
A trigger in your existing routine, Morning coffee	A small, specific habit tied to that cue, Write one sentence	A small win that reinforces the behavior, Checkmark on your to-do list	A simple way to monitor your progress, Log it in a notebook or app

For example, if you want to become a better speaker, you might use your lunch break as a cue, practice speaking for one minute as the action, feel a boost of confidence as the reward, and track your progress in a journal. Over time, these small steps add up and silence the internal voices that once doubted your abilities.

ACTION PROMPT: **BUILD YOUR ANCHOR**

Pick a goal and define:

- Cue (e.g., after breakfast)

....

....

....

- Action (e.g., a 10-minute walk)

....

....

....

- Reward (e.g., a sense of accomplishment)

....

....

....

- Track (e.g., in an app)

....

....

....

Start today and document it as your first vote for who you are becoming.

You're Already Becoming Someone

Without even realizing it, your current habits are already sculpting your future self. Every repeated behavior contributes to your identity, gradually shaping the person you will become. The key question is: do these habits align with the person you aspire to be?

Changing your life isn't about dramatic overhauls overnight. It's about adjusting your trajectory one intentional, tiny habit at a time. Each decision you make nudges your future just a little bit. As weeks and months pass, those small shifts accumulate until one day, and you recognize that you're no longer dreaming of your new identity; you have become it.

Your future is determined not by occasional grand gestures but by the sum of your daily habits. The good news is that you can start reshaping that future right now.

Before we dive into more tactical strategies in the next chapter, take a moment to reflect: Who do you want to become, and what small, simple ritual can you start today that will cast your first vote for that identity? Don't wait for motivation or clarity. Act in a small, consistent way right now, and let that be the foundation of your future.

Because ultimately, your life doesn't need massive, sudden shifts to change dramatically. It requires daily, intentional choices, quiet actions that, over time, build an identity aligned with your aspirations.

YOUR HABITS ARE EVERYTHING. AND TODAY, YOU HAVE THE POWER TO CHOOSE THEM.

03

BECOMING WHO YOU NEED TO BE

"

CONFIDENCE ISN'T
AN INHERENT
CHARACTERISTIC;
IT'S LIKE A RECEIPT
THAT PROVES YOU
EARNED IT.

"

CHAPTER 8

Confidence Is Constructed, Not Inborn

"You must do the thing you think you cannot do."

— ELEANOR ROOSEVELT

The Myth of Innate Confidence

I once looked at those who exuded confidence with envy, not mere admiration, but a deep, bitter longing. They made everything appear effortless, didn't they? The smooth talker at networking events, the friend who effortlessly lit up every room, the colleague who pitched ideas to even the most skeptical audiences without hesitation. It seemed as if confidence was woven into their DNA, a golden ticket granted at birth to life's exclusive club.

I believed they possessed something I lacked, an intrinsic, unteachable quality, whether it was charisma, charm, or pure daring. That feeling of absence left me quietly holding back in situations where I had valuable insights, shrinking in the presence of those who intimidated me, and keeping ideas to myself because I doubted, I had the "it" factor to present them.

Then, one afternoon, at a workshop where I felt undeserving of attendance, a woman named Carla reframed everything with one unexpected sentence.

"Confidence isn't a trait," she said casually, "it's a receipt."

A receipt? I paused, puzzled. I had always thought of confidence as something you either possessed or didn't, similar to height or eye color. But a receipt implied evidence, something earned and tangible: a record of your actions rather than an unchangeable birthright.

Carla's words settled into my mind, gently shaking the foundations of what I thought I knew. If confidence were a receipt, then it was something you could collect. And if you could build it over time, perhaps I wasn't as broken or unqualified as I'd believed. I was simply in the early stages of gathering proof.

I Didn't Wake Up Confident

The first invitation to speak at a major industry event should have filled me with confidence. I had dedicated years to getting ready for that moment. I knew my material well, had rehearsed repeatedly, and even had the blessing of a mentor. Yet confidence was nowhere to be found on the morning of the event.

Instead, a tight dread wrapped around my chest. My pulse raced as I scanned the hundreds of expectant yet indifferent faces waiting for me to step up. As my speaking time drew nearer, my inner voice grew louder with doubts:

"They'll see right through you." "You're going to embarrass yourself." "You're not ready for this."

Backstage, in that overwhelming moment, I realized something vital: it wasn't a matter of lacking skill or preparation but the mistaken idea that confidence must show up before you act, like an entry fee granting permission to proceed.

Then clarity struck: confidence isn't the entry fee; it's the reward you earn by moving forward despite your fear.

To be clear, I didn't feel heroic on that stage. I stumbled through my introduction, and my voice cracked under pressure, but I got through it. That night, rather than writing "I nailed it," I simply recorded, "Did it anyway."

That's when it hit me: confidence often feels more like the sensation of surviving than of triumphing. You might not leave the stage feeling invincible; you might just feel relieved it's over. And that relief, that data point, is proof in its own way.

The Lie: I'll Feel Ready Someday

We all harbor a little lie: that someday, somehow, we'll feel ready. This idea can be seductive and equally destructive. It disguises itself as patience or perfect timing, but it's simply avoidance wrapped in the guise of self-care. It's a fear hidden behind a pretense of waiting for certainty.

Maybe for you, it's the promotion you keep delaying applying for, the difficult conversation you keep postponing, the exciting project you never launch, or even the vulnerable act of reaching out to someone you admire. It isn't your ability that holds you back; it's the flawed belief that readiness will eventually appear in a perfectly packaged form.

The truth is that you're waiting for the green light of emotional permission. But here's the inconvenient fact: confidence is seldom the starting point.

You don't wait until you feel confident to act; you act, and confidence builds.

That readiness lie traps you in a cycle: you don't act because you don't feel confident, and you can't feel confident until you act. So you wait, rehearse, prep, and tweak endlessly, inadvertently building a case against yourself instead of building resilience.

Here's where you need to shift gears: stop treating confidence as a precondition. Instead, view it as a byproduct, a natural consequence of doing what terrifies you, even as it continues to terrify you.

After all, those who appear confident didn't wait until they felt prepared. They simply moved first, and confidence followed like a faithful shadow.

The Trap: The Readiness Illusion

Here's a difficult truth: waiting to feel ready is a losing game. Confidence isn't the green light you imagine; it isn't a permission slip or an internal signal that says, "Now is the time."

It's not the spark that motivates action; it's the outcome of taking action.

The readiness illusion tempts you by promising that you'll be ready once you feel calm, prepared, and centered. Instead, you end up stalling, accumulating more information, and getting caught in a loop of analysis instead of doing.

Over time, that hesitation can become part of your identity. You begin to say, "I'm just not confident," wearing that label as if it were true. Yet, it's not who you are; it's simply where you paused along the way.

The idea that you need to feel certain before starting only convinces you further that you're unqualified. The reality, however, is that most people doing remarkable things are doing them while feeling uncertain, second-guessing themselves, and constantly wondering, "Who allowed me in here?"

Readiness isn't the starting block; it's the reward. The longer you delay, the more distant that feeling becomes because confidence is built in the doing and repeated practice.

So next time you find yourself waiting for a surge of confidence, ask, "What evidence can I create today?" That question shifts the power back into your hands.

THE FRAMEWORK: **THE CONFIDENCE CODE**

Confidence isn't something you stumble upon; it's something you file away and document. It isn't discovered by accident; it's constructed deliberately, much like any good system.

The Confidence Code is a four-step loop you can rely on whenever fear tries to dictate your actions. It transforms confidence from an elusive trait into a process, a rhythm rather than an anomaly.

1. Act Before You Feel Ready

This is the hardest step, but it's non-negotiable: action always comes before assurance. You won't feel confident until after you've taken that step, so do it regardless. Courage is not a feeling; it's a decision, a committed movement. The only way out of fear is to move through it.

2. Record What You Did

Right after you act, document the moment. Don't let it fade away into your memory. Write it down, record a voice note, or enter it into your favorite app. This becomes your receipt, your concrete evidence, because our brains tend to forget even our own victories.

3. Revisit What You Survived

If you don't periodically review your triumphs, confidence will diminish. Revisiting your wins trains your nervous system to sense safety even during challenges. It teaches your mind, "We've been here before; we survived and learned." Let these memories strengthen you.

4. Repeat With Less Hesitation

This is where the loop transforms into a ladder. Each repetition builds on the last, gradually diminishing the need for pep talks and replacing them with habit. Confidence compounds over time; your personal file grows thicker, and your fear becomes thinner. You become unshakable by filing away proof rather than waiting for permission.

System Building: The Confidence Ledger

Now, let's turn these ideas into a habit.

You've likely heard of keeping a gratitude journal, but this is different. This is a courage journal, a record of your risks and moments when fear didn't win. We call it the Confidence Ledger. Once you start building it, your self-doubt won't stand a chance.

Imagine confidence as a growing file cabinet rather than a sudden flash of lightning. Every time you face a fear and live to tell the tale, consider it a receipt: a documented moment that shouts, "I did it despite being scared."

Here's how to begin:

■ Create a dedicated space using the medium that suits your life: a journal, a spreadsheet, a notes app, or even a private voice memo collection. It doesn't matter where; what matters is that it exists.

■ Log your evidence: after each courageous act, whether big or small, note three things:

- What scared you

- What you did anyway

- What the outcome was (regardless of success)

■ Revisit your entries weekly: read them at the end of each week. Don't merely collect receipts, study them. Notice how your story evolves, your voice grows stronger, and your willingness to take risks compounds over time.

The Confidence Ledger is not about garnering public accolades or viral moments. It's grounded in private acts of bravery and quiet audacity that, over time, rewire your self-perception, not because others told you so, but because your record of achievements proves it.

ACTION PROMPT: **START YOUR CONFIDENCE LEDGER**

Open a blank page and title it "I've Done Harder Things Before."

Write down three moments, big or small, when you acted despite not feeling ready. For each moment, answer:

- What scared you?

- What did you do regardless?

- How did you feel afterward?

Don't overthink it; this exercise is about gathering evidence, not crafting perfect outcomes. Let this page serve as your proof because confidence isn't magic; it's memory, and you've already earned more than you realize.

Let's make this practical.

Take a fresh page in your journal, notes app, or Google Doc, and label it "I've Done Harder Things Before." This is where you begin to document what's already true: you've faced challenges, survived fear, and taken action despite uncertainty. Now, name those moments.

Your task is simple:

- Write down three instances, regardless of their scale, where you took action even though you didn't feel ready.

- For each, answer:

- What scared me?

- What did I do anyway?

- How did I feel afterward?

Don't censor your thoughts. Even if the moment feels trivial, speaking up in a meeting, sending that email you revised multiple times, or making a daunting call, they all count.

This exercise isn't about performance but recognizing and building patterns. Your goal is to compile evidence to refer back to when fear roars. And when it does (and it will), you'll have an ever-growing reminder that whispers, "I've done harder things before," because you have, and you will again.

Confidence doesn't announce itself with a knock on your door or parade in with banners and balloons declaring, "Now's your time." It doesn't mirror back at you in perfection. It isn't magical. Rather, it manifests as a movement: the shaky hands sending that email, the moment you hit "submit" even when your stomach churns, or walking into a room where you feel unprepared yet choosing to sit down anyway.

Confidence isn't born from waiting; it's built from witnessing yourself repeatedly confronting what scares you and realizing that you're still standing, breathing, and growing despite it all. So, stop waiting to feel ready. Instead, start logging your actions. File your receipts. Let fear be your cue instead of your stop sign. Allow the evidence of your bravery to drown out the doubts.

Remember: confidence isn't something you're born with; it's something you construct over time. You're not behind; you're simply in the process of becoming. Act first, and let confidence follow.

"

DISCOMFORT
ISN'T YOUR
ADVERSARY IT'S
THE GATEWAY.

"

CHAPTER 9

How Comfort Is Robbing Your Potential

"Life begins at the end of your comfort zone."

— NEALE DONALD WALSCH

The Quiet Killer

Comfort never bursts onto the scene, demanding action. It doesn't blare like failure or bellow like fear. Instead, it murmurs, almost imperceptibly, slowly convincing you that taking your time is smart, that standing still is secure, and that "later" equates to maturity.

Left unchecked, comfort gradually becomes a stealthy killer, not murdering your body but dulling your edge, dimming your spark, and halting your expansion. It whispers, "You've done enough for now," long before you truly have, and lures you into extended rest when deep down you know growth is painful.

That's the peril: comfort masquerades as responsibility, self-care, and balance. Until one day, you realize you're not progressing but merely lurking in a well-furnished waiting room.

The Moment I Opted for the Easy Path

I recall a time I rarely mention; it still stings whenever I think about it. Several years ago, I was invited to participate in a leadership and risk panel. I had prepared extensively; I possessed the insights and stories I knew would resonate. Yet, the idea of stepping onto that stage, standing next to seasoned executives and experts, filled me with unease.

I convinced myself I needed more time, and my brand wasn't "ready" for that kind of spotlight. I told myself I shouldn't speak on a subject I hadn't mastered yet. So, I declined.

And the opportunity passed.

The spot went to someone else, not necessarily more prepared, but certainly less intimidated by showing up in the middle of growth, someone who understood that an imperfect presence beats staying hidden in the shadows.

That memory doesn't haunt me because I lost an opportunity, but because I now see that I turned it down not for strategic reasons but simply because comfort triumphed in that moment. I've since learned that the more you indulge in comfort, the louder its demands become.

The Myth: "If It Feels Hard, It Must Be Wrong"

We live in a society that praises ease, using buzzwords like "flow," "alignment," and "feeling good about your choices." This can be useful for protecting your energy from burnout, but it also provides an excuse to dodge challenges.

In our culture, we've mistakenly equated friction with failure.

As soon as something becomes difficult, we view it as a warning, a red flag, or even a sign from the universe that it isn't meant for us. But bear in mind that discomfort isn't always dysfunctional. Sometimes, discomfort indicates you're in the gym of life, your identity is being challenged, and your nervous system is stepping into unfamiliar territory. You're not off course; you just need a little more practice.

If you wait for things to feel easy again before you move, you'll create a life that may seem safe but ultimately feels confined.

The Reality: Growth Always Comes with Friction

If you've ever started a new exercise regimen, learned a new skill, or walked into a room of intimidating individuals, you know that growth rarely feels like clarity; it feels chaotic.

You'll find yourself second-guessing, feeling like an impostor. Your chest may tighten, your thoughts may spiral, and every part of you might try to retreat to what's familiar. That reaction isn't a warning sign; it's merely your body's response to growth. Your brain, particularly your amygdala, is wired to interpret uncertainty and risk as threats. Because growth often requires embracing both, your nervous system naturally triggers alarms. That flinch you experience isn't a sign of failure but feedback. It means you're stretching boundaries, breaking old loops, and teaching your body a new way to function. If things feel awkward, shaky, or vulnerable, chances are you're on the right path.

"DISCOMFORT IS A COMPASS. IT DOESN'T ALWAYS SIGNAL DANGER; SOMETIMES, IT DIRECTS YOU TOWARD YOUR DESTINY."

The Overuse of "Alignment"

Let's address a common buzzword in self-help circles: "alignment." Too often, people use alignment as a free pass to avoid growth. Comments like, "It didn't feel aligned, so I passed," or "I want to wait until it feels aligned," or even "That project didn't feel expansive" have become all too common. But here's a truth that rarely gets mentioned: true alignment can feel uneasy at first. It isn't meant to feel effortless; it's akin to wearing a new skin that fits better than your old one but still needs time to settle.

What many label as "misalignment" is essentially resistance, a bodily reaction against expansion. So, the next time you catch yourself saying, "This doesn't feel aligned," ask: Is it truly at odds with my values, or is it merely at odds with what feels comfortable? Only one of those should have your attention.

Discomfort as Information

Not every painful feeling is productive, and not every moment of discomfort signals danger. There's a kind of pain that's destructive: when your boundaries are crossed, your values are dismissed, or your well-being is compromised. Then there's a constructive kind of discomfort: when your skills are tested, your identity is expanded, and your excuses are challenged. Understanding the difference is crucial.

Consider this simple breakdown:

Discomfort Type

How It Feels

Likely Meaning

Shrinking Pain

Tightness, shutdown

Your voice is being silenced, or your truth is compromised

Stretching Pain

Tension, exposure, alertness

You're growing into a new version of yourself, embracing risk or a new role.

Stretching pain might manifest as saying "yes" even before feeling "ready," sharing your work despite imperfections, applying for a role that scares you, or initiating a conversation that could change everything.

This kind of discomfort isn't a cue to withdraw; it's an invitation to work through the resistance and move forward.

On the far side of that tension lies the transformation.

The Opportunity I Nearly Missed

A few years back, I received an email that made my heart pound.

It was an invitation to speak on a panel. It was a modest opportunity, yet significant to me, centered around leadership, decision-making, and identity.

I read it, reread it, and almost immediately crafted a polite refusal.

Why?

Because I wasn't "ready." I had never spoken on a panel before. I doubted whether my voice could hold its own among others. In its usual pattern before growth, my brain convinced me to shrink.

And I nearly accepted that story.

I almost surrendered to comfort, almost passed up an opportunity that could stretch me simply because it didn't feel easy.

Then, a close friend said, "You're not refusing this because it isn't the right fit; you're refusing it because you're scared of not appearing perfect."

That struck me hard.

She was right. My discomfort wasn't a warning but proof that I needed to step up.

So I went ahead. I showed up, my voice trembled, and I filled the space with too many "ums." Yet afterward, two women approached me, saying, "You voiced exactly what I had been feeling but couldn't express."

That moment resonated deeply, not for its perfection but its raw authenticity.

It changed something inside me.

The Comfort Tax

No one talks about this: comfort comes at a price. We often treat comfort as a reward, something earned and deserved. But what if comfort isn't neutral? What if every time you choose the familiar over the risky, every time you opt for safety over growth, you're paying an unseen tax?

This invisible fee shows up later as:

A persistent feeling that you're meant for more, a backlog of half-finished ideas, a twinge of envy toward those who took the plunge, or a nagging awareness that while life might seem "fine," it lacks true fulfillment. Comfort isn't a reward; it's a trap. And the longer you remain in it, the higher the cost becomes.

From Comfort to Courage: A Practical Framework

It's one thing to hear "step outside your comfort zone," but what does that look like in everyday life? It's not on a grand stage or during a major career pivot, but on an ordinary Tuesday when your heart pounds even though the stakes aren't monumental.

One tool I rely on is the Stretch Scale:

Zone Description: What It Looks Like

■ **Green Zone:** The Comfort Zone: routine, predictable Boredom, security, checking emails, binge-watching shows

■ **Yellow Zone:** The Stretch Zone: a gentle nudge toward growth Mild discomfort, alertness, starting that long-delayed conversation

■ **Red Zone:** The Stress Zone: overwhelming and paralyzing Panic, freezing, and anxiety from taking on too much at once

The aim isn't to jump straight from green to red; that leads to burnout, but to dwell in the yellow zone, gradually training yourself to accept discomfort as a regular part of growth.

Discomfort Into Strength

Instead of constantly seeking motivation, we need little proof that discomfort isn't our enemy. That's the essence of discomfort training:

deliberately choosing small stretches that remind your nervous system, "This is safe. I can handle this. I'm growing."

I set a challenge for myself: one new stretch every day. Nothing monumental, just something slightly out of your comfort zone. Sometimes, it was posting a video without obsessing over every detail. Other times, it meant initiating a difficult conversation or speaking up in a meeting when silence felt easier.

This isn't about bravery; it's about rewiring your instinct to retreat at the first sign of discomfort. Remember: discomfort isn't the enemy; it's the bridge to growth.

Talia's Turning Point

Talia was no stranger to leadership. Having managed small teams successfully for years, when a new VP role opened up her organization, she froze. It wasn't that she didn't desire the position; it was that being in the spotlight scared her. "It's not that I doubt my capabilities," she confessed during our strategy session, "it's that I fear being exposed while learning." Terrified of revealing imperfections under scrutiny, she hesitated, delaying her decision for three weeks.

I asked her, "Which is scarier, staying stuck in discomfort or being in the same position a year from now?"

After a pause, she softly admitted, "Same spot, without a doubt."

That question flipped her perspective.

Talia went ahead and applied. Though she didn't land the job, something shifted permanently. She stopped viewing discomfort as a sign of unreadiness and started embracing it as evidence of evolution.

That setback didn't break her; it emboldened her. Six months later, she received an even better offer, one she'd never pursued if she'd clung to comfort.

Why We Often Remain Stuck

It's not laziness that holds most people back; comfort is easier to justify.

It's simpler to say, "I'm staying where it's safe," than admit, "I'm scared to grow." It's easier to claim, "I'm still weighing my options," than to confess, "I fear being exposed." It's much simpler to scroll endlessly than face the awkwardness of imperfect action.

We've come to see the comfort zone as a responsible state, but the longer you linger there, the more your world shrinks.

Remember: discomfort isn't the opposite of safety; it's the tuition fee for growth.

Your 3-Day Discomfort Sprint

Over the next three days, choose one small, challenging task each day. That's all. It should be:

- Just uncomfortable enough
- Slightly visible to others
- A small step against your routine

For example, say no to something that drains you, share an idea without over-editing, or ask for feedback you've been dodging. Keep a log of these "Discomfort Wins."

By gradually building your tolerance for discomfort, you create a pathway to all the opportunities you've been postponing.

Why We Chase Ease (and Its Hidden Costs)

Let's be honest: you don't always seek comfort simply because it feels good, it's familiar.

Your brain's top priority is survival; it sticks with what it knows will keep you safe. Even if that familiarity is dull, unfulfilling, or slowly stifles your potential, your brain's homeostatic resistance pushes you away from change because it views the unknown as dangerous.

So even as you strive to grow, your nervous system quietly advises, "Let's wait until we're more prepared. Let's not make waves now. Let's stick with what we know."

This isn't about laziness; it's your brain's way of clinging to an old identity.

Rewiring Your Comfort Reflex

If you want to broaden your life, you must broaden your sense of safety.

That doesn't mean ignoring fear but reprogramming your brain's associations with safety.

Safety doesn't equate to ease; it's about making deliberate choices. Once you begin choosing discomfort on purpose, your nervous system gradually learns that there's nothing to fear.

Soon, you stop flinching, retreating, and confusing challenges with danger.

That's when you reclaim your power.

Because suddenly, the hard things no longer seem insurmountable; they feel like a familiar part of your journey.

The Shift From Comfort to Capability

Here's a mental shift that transformed my life:

Every time you avoid discomfort, you train your body to retreat. Every time you confront it, you prepare yourself for greater challenges.

Discomfort isn't evidence of failure; it's evidence that you're training for something bigger.

Think about it:

The first time you spoke up in a meeting, it was terrifying. The fifth time, it felt normal. The tenth time, it felt like leadership.

You never eliminated the discomfort; instead, you built your capacity to handle it.

That's the shift that changes your trajectory. It isn't about making things feel effortless but acting even when they don't.

LISA'S LEAP: **A CASE STUDY**

Lisa had been freelancing for three years, enjoying a solid income, good clients, and total autonomy. Yet, she kept circling the idea of building something larger: a content agency, a team, or a brand beyond solo work.

Every time we talked, she found new reasons to wait: "This isn't the right season," "I need to refine my offerings first," or "I'll revisit it once I hit a specific revenue mark."

In reality, she was addicted to comfort.

She cherished being the top performer, staying in control, and knowing what to expect. Scaling up meant letting go, delegating, risking public mistakes, and admitting she didn't have all the answers.

Eventually, she hit an emotional wall. It wasn't burnout from overwork but from ignoring her true desires.

So she challenged herself: commit to one thing each week that scares you into growth.

She launched a podcast, began hiring slowly, and launched projects before they felt perfect.

It wasn't smooth, but it reawakened her. The discomfort didn't destroy her; it built her, expanding her business, capacity, and sense of self.

GROWTH BEGINS THE MOMENT YOU'RE WILLING TO BE SEEN BEFORE YOU FEEL READY.

COMFORT ZONE AUDIT: **UNCOVERING HIDDEN PATTERNS**

Take a moment for a gut check. Grab your journal or notes app and answer these three questions honestly, without judgment:

1. In which areas of your life does it feel too quiet, like the conversations you avoid, the ideas you never share, or the boundaries you never set?

2. What have you settled for as "fine," when in reality, fine is just code for comfort, a silent graveyard for potential?

3. Where have you prioritized control over growth, where you're coasting on what has always worked rather than stretching into new territories?

Remember: if everything in your life feels 100% manageable, it might very well be 0% transformative.

Your Growth Exposure Plan

Discomfort without direction leads to burnout, but structured discomfort sparks transformation. Here's a three-step plan to intentionally stretch your boundaries without chaos:

Step 1: Identify Your Next Growth Challenge

This isn't your greatest fear; it's simply the next challenge that could gently shift your boundaries. Ask yourself, "What would make me mildly uncomfortable without leaving me paralyzed?" Consider something small that makes your heart race and raises your standards, like sending that email, speaking frankly in a meeting, or sharing an idea before it's completely polished.

Step 2: Schedule the Stretch

Don't wait for courage to appear. Block out time on your calendar for that single 15-minute action or one decisive step. Focus on frequency over perfection and make these stretches routine rather than heroic.

Step 3: Reflect Without Judgment

After taking your stretch, ask yourself: What did I feel? What did I fear? What actually happened? The aim isn't flawless execution; it's proof that you survived (and perhaps even thrived) despite the discomfort. Over time, this routine desensitizes your fear by demonstrating that there's nothing inherently dangerous about stepping into the unknown.

ACTION PROMPT: **THE DISCOMFORT REPS LOG**

For the next seven days, choose one thing each day that unsettles you just a bit. Do it quickly, if possible, in public. Log what you did and how it felt, just like you'd record your progress in a workout. Because that's exactly what it is: a rep for boosting your capacity for growth. Treat discomfort like a muscle; instead of fearing it, train with it.

Shifting from Safety to Self-Trust

We've been conditioned to believe that comfort equals peace. But true peace isn't the absence of discomfort but the presence of alignment, even if achieving that means embracing a bit of unease.

Think back: remember Michelle? She didn't wait for comfort to settle in. She acted even when it was missing, and that action reshaped her understanding of what she was capable of.

That possibility is here for you now, before you feel fully confident and receive applause or complete clarity. You're not meant to wait until you feel ready; you're meant to move forward and let readiness come with the journey.

REMEMBER,
COMFORT
IS SIMPLE,
BUT GROWTH
IS EARNED.
CHOOSE WISELY.

"

DISCIPLINE IS
CHOOSING WHAT
YOU WANT MOST
OVER WHAT YOU
WANT NOW.

"

CHAPTER 10

Consistency Beats Talent Every Time

"It's not what you do once in a while that shapes your life, but what you do consistently."

— TONY ROBBINS

The Illusion of Talent

Let's be clear: raw talent is overrated. Not that it doesn't matter; it just isn't what drives you across the finish line. In every field, from cyber-security teams to creative startups, I've watched people with natural gifts burn out, not because they weren't brilliant but because they lacked consistency. Meanwhile, those who weren't the most flashy quietly rose to the top through regular, repeated effort. Talent might catch your eye, but consistency builds unstoppable momentum.

For years, I believed I had to wait for the perfect moment: the right burst of energy, the flash of inspiration, that perfect uninterrupted block of time. It made sense. Why force progress when you could ride the wave when you felt on? I became excellent at imagining my potential yet terrible at proving it. My creative projects would start and then fade away; my ideas were strong in theory but weak in execution, and my fitness routine was intense for a couple of weeks, then vanished for months. One day, I looked at my calendar and realized I wasn't actually tired; I was simply chasing fleeting bursts of momentum.

It took years to understand that your best output isn't born from sheer inspiration but from habit. Think of everyone you admire in your field, every transformation you respect, every writer you quote. They didn't create success only when they felt amazing. The secret was showing up even on the days they didn't. The real difference isn't in who is the most talented; it's in who builds the muscle of showing up every day.

A Friend Who Wasn't the Star

Let me tell you about Anita. She wasn't the type to dominate a room or steal the spotlight. Quiet and polite, she often felt uncertain in group discussions but never skipped a beat. Anita wasn't the fastest learner or the one with the natural "wow" factor. Instead, she built quiet, steady progress through simple, repeated actions. Each day, she logged in, completed her tasks, asked meaningful questions, and returned the next day ready to do it all over again. Within three months, her consistency transformed her into a formidable force, not because she was the flashiest, but because she was the most reliable. That quiet perseverance, that daily commitment, is the real cheat code.

We tend to overestimate what we can achieve in a week and underestimate the impact of showing up every day for an entire year. Small, everyday actions compound over time. One workout can lead to a transformation; one pitch can gradually build a robust pipeline; one post can develop into a powerful brand. These results aren't glamorous bursts of brilliance; they are the inevitable outcome of routines that work. As I always say, "If your action is inconsistent, your outcomes will always feel unpredictable."

What Anita discovered in practice; neuroscience now confirms in our brains.

So what? That quiet consistency outpaces fleeting brilliance, so let's see how your brain rewards repetition.

The Neuroscience of Repetition: Why Consistency Works

Your brain is wired for efficiency; it prefers predictable routines over constant effort. Every time you perform a behavior, however mundane, you strengthen the neural pathways associated with it. Imagine carving a path in a forest: the more you walk it, the clearer the trail becomes. That's why habits start as challenges and eventually become automatic. It isn't about mustering extra discipline; it's about making actions easy to repeat through strategic automation. The best doesn't ask, "Do I feel like it today?" because they've already removed that question from their process.

Success isn't about possessing more discipline but creating environments that make the right choices easier. If you want to read more, keep a book by your bed. If you want to write every day, leave your document open on your desktop. If you want to eat healthier, stock your fridge with nutritious options. These aren't acts of extreme willpower; they're designs intentionally built into your environment. I often remind myself, "Discipline is the result of decisions you made yesterday." The people you admire don't wield more willpower; they've crafted systems that protect their priorities.

Ask yourself: are you chasing the quick rush of progress or building habits that create lasting change? The thrill of a quick win is enticing; the dopamine hit from a burst of achievement or recognition. But that excitement is fleeting. What works is the routine: the daily check-in, that regular writing session, the consistent work, and even the early bedtime. Consistency might not feel glamorous, but it reshapes who you are fundamentally.

Armed with that understanding, the next step is designing a failproof routine, so you never have to 'will' yourself again.

So what? Knowing how your neural pathways strengthen means you can stop relying on willpower and start shaping your environment. If discipline is a byproduct of design, then your next move is to architect a routine that runs itself.

The Daily Rhythm Builder

Here's a simple framework for building unstoppable consistency, even on your worst days. I call it the D.R.I.P. Method:

D = Define your anchor. Identify one small action that signals, "I'm on track today" (for example, opening your document or putting on your workout clothes).

R = Remove resistance. Figure out what makes your routine harder than it needs to be (like a cluttered desk or an overwhelming goal).

I = Initiate before emotion. Start the habit before waiting to "feel like it."

P = Protect the streak. Log your action, celebrate the win, and commit to not breaking the chain, even if it's by just a day.

This isn't about chasing productivity fads but safeguarding your performance with proven systems.

STORY: **HOW CONSISTENCY QUIETLY WINS**

I once worked with a consultant named Lina. She didn't have a flashy social media strategy or a viral content plan. Instead, she made one simple promise: "Every weekday, I'll reach out to one potential client or collaborator." Even on days when she didn't feel inspired, she stuck to her routine. Over time, those small daily actions added to 240 targeted touches in a year. The result? Not only did her business grow, but she also became a trusted name in her niche. It wasn't about making noise; it was about the quiet power of consistent action.

REFLECTION PROMPT: **AUDIT YOUR DROP**

Think of one goal you're pursuing. Ask yourself:

- What simple behavior shows that you're moving forward?
- What obstacles can you remove today?
- How can you protect this routine for the next 30 days?

Write it down: "Progress is built in drops, not waves."

The Real Secret: Get Boring on Purpose

If you're forever chasing the allure of new and exciting routines, you'll never develop the depth needed for lasting change. We live in a culture that prizes novelty: new hacks, routines, and methods to optimize ourselves. While a bit of novelty can jumpstart a behavior, the boring, repeated actions truly build growth. Repetition might not be exciting, but it brings reliability. In short, you will not reach your most ambitious goals unless you are willing to embrace the ordinary. In this case, boredom isn't a sign of failure; it's a sign that you're doing the work of mastery.

No matter how committed you are, you will miss a day here or there. Life gets in the way, such as illness, unexpected events, or simply a slip-up. These moments aren't failures; they are part of being human. What counts is your ability to bounce back quickly. When you falter, remind yourself: "You don't need a perfect streak. You need a fast recovery." Here's a quick blueprint for getting back on track:

■ Spot the story: Recognize the negative narrative that follows a slip, like "I always mess up."

■ Break the pattern: Ensure you don't go another day without your anchor habit, even if it's only for a minute.

■ Shrink the shame: One miss is life; two become a pattern. Interrupt it before it does.

■ Return to the ritual: Reclaim your habit by returning to your established cue and making the action as accessible as possible.

Remember, success isn't about never slipping up but how quickly you get back in the game.

The One Habit That Saved My Momentum

There was a time when everything in my life felt like it was crumbling. Overwhelming work, sleepless nights, and mounting deadlines had me skipping my usual routines, writing, working out, and all the habits I'd built up began to unravel. In those moments, the inner critic shouted, "You're inconsistent. You can't keep anything up." Instead of surrendering to that voice, I got up, opened a new note, and wrote one paragraph. That tiny act wasn't about making giant leaps but proving to myself that I hadn't given up. From then on, whenever things got tough, I committed to doing one small thing, no matter how insignificant it felt. That simple rule became my lifeline.

Consistency Is a Compounding Machine

Consider this: if you dedicate just 10 minutes a day for a year, that amounts to 3,650 minutes of focused work, be it writing, learning, creating, or practicing a skill. That's 60 hours of deliberate action, built steadily without overexertion. Now imagine applying that same principle across different areas of your life: your health, mind, and career. Consistency isn't about doing the most in a day but enduring over time. As I like to say, "The people who win aren't the ones who do the most. They're the ones who do it longest."

Build a Life Around Repeatable Wins

What's more powerful than a burst of hustle? It's a system that carries you through even on your worst days. We often overestimate our peak performance while underestimating what can be achieved by simply not stopping. Think about it: what is your "bad day" version of your habit? What's the smallest action you can take that still counts as progress? Imagine designing your day so you're still moving forward, even on low-energy days. This is how you build lasting consistency, not by trying to be superhuman, but by setting a high baseline that doesn't rely solely on willpower.

REFLECTION PROMPT: **THE RECOVERY MUSCLE**

Reflect on a habit you abandoned because you "messed up once." What was the story you told yourself about that lapse? How could you redefine your rule, for example, "Never miss two days in a row?" Write it down: "I don't need perfect. I need recovery."

....

....

....

....

The Invisible Force Behind Every Transformation

True change rarely feels dramatic. It's subtle, like brushing your teeth instead of scrolling through social media, writing when no one is watching, or lacing up your shoes in the early morning when no one sees. The most powerful changes are quiet and incremental. If you're waiting for transformation to feel dramatic, you'll miss the small victories unfolding each day. Consistency is the slowest form of magic, but it's the only kind that works.

Who You Become When No One's Watching

Your true self isn't defined by what you share with the world; it's revealed by what you do when no one is clapping or checking in. The habits you build quietly in the background are the ones that truly shape your identity. Consistent actions prove that you're evolving, regardless of external validation. When you understand this, you'll stop needing hype and start valuing the power of another rep.

The Identity Loop

Let's wrap up with a practical ritual, a way to cement your evolving identity with each small habit:

1. Pick a 5-minute identity habit (like meditating, writing, reaching out, stretching, or reviewing your budget).

2. Choose a consistent cue (after coffee, before bed, post-shower, after school drop-off).

3. Verbally affirm your identity: say, "I'm doing this because I'm a [writer, athlete, creator, etc.]."

4. Mark the win by checking it off on your habit tracker. That checkmark isn't just a symbol on paper; it's a vote cast in your favor.

Repeat this daily, track your progress weekly, and celebrate monthly. Over time, these small actions create a powerful vote for the person you're becoming.

REFLECTION PROMPT: **WHO ARE YOU VOTING FOR THIS WEEK?**

Take a minute to ask yourself: what identity are you voting for this week? What is one small action that proves it? What system can you set up so that you repeat it every day? Write it down and remind yourself: "I don't need more talent. I need more reps." Remember, you're not just building habits; you're building who you are.

04

REAL-LIFE PROOF AND PITFALL NAVIGATION

"

THE ONLY
DIFFERENCE
BETWEEN YOU AND
THE PEOPLE YOU
ADMIRE IS THAT
THEY STOPPED
WAITING FOR
PERMISSION.

"

CHAPTER 11

Why Not Being Special Sets You Free

The Myth of Specialness

When you look up to people who share their wins online, launch businesses, or deliver powerful ideas, it might seem they're born with a secret formula for confidence and success. But here's the truth: they aren't magically gifted. They weren't born with a confidence gene or handed a clear road map. They were scared, doubted themselves, and faced chaos like you. Yet, they moved forward despite it all.

I used to admire these individuals with a mix of awe and envy. I remember attending a conference where a speaker commanded the room with a steady voice and a well-crafted story. At that moment, I heard my inner critic whisper, "She's naturally talented; you're not." But over coffee later, she admitted that she had been terrified too, that her inner voice told her, "No one cares." Still, she spoke up and proved her ability through action.

Later, I watched a community leader organize local cleanups, and my inner guardian warned, "She's fearless; you're not." But she, too, had faced early doubts, starting with a single event before building her credentials.

Maybe you've felt it too, admiring a chef's experimental pop-up dinners or a parent who handles chaos with calm authority. That part of you whispers that you're "not built like them." But they took action while you waited for a moment to feel worthy. Their success isn't born from perfection; it's the result of facing fears and moving forward. And you're capable of that, too, starting right now.

So what? Real confidence isn't inherited; it's earned through imperfect action.

If confidence isn't magic, then waiting for it is a fool's errand; so let's uncover the real trap.

The Trap of Waiting for Permission

Waiting for the perfect moment or someone else's approval is a trap. Our brains are wired to highlight risks: fear of rejection, fear of failure, and these risks get amplified by the three voices inside us. One voice says, "You're not qualified." Another urges, "Wait until everything is perfect." And the third whispers, "Why bother?" When you're waiting for permission, you're essentially waiting for certainty that will never come.

Early in my career, I watched peers pitch their ideas while I stayed silent, held back by the fear of appearing foolish. I thought I needed to master every skill and get a sign that I was ready. Once, I missed a speaking slot at a summit because my inner critic convinced me that my talk wasn't polished enough. I waited until someone else took the opportunity, and that reinforced the message that I was always one step behind. The real trap wasn't my ability; it was waiting for that elusive permission.

Maybe you're putting off a family goal, an art project, or even a chance at a promotion because you believe you need to be "perfect" first. Instead of waiting to feel worthy, take that first small step. Every single action you take builds a little more self-efficacy. As Dr. Albert Bandura points out, each success, however small, rewires your brain and shows you that what really matters is movement.

The Power of Being Seen

People start to notice when you show up consistently, even in small, quiet ways. Your repeated actions build credibility over time. Dr. B.J. Fogg's work on behavior change tells us that small wins trigger dopamine, reinforcing the habit of action. Showing up isn't about grand gestures; it's about proving to yourself repeatedly that you're committed to progress. Take Talia's story. I met her at a networking event where she mostly stayed on the fringe, almost invisible. Yet, during a breakout session, she mentioned her side business digitizing intake forms for therapists. Her inner voices had warned her, "You're too small; no one cares." Early on, her clients were few, and her self-doubt was strong. But she kept going. One win led to another; she earned referrals and built credibility, not through loud declarations, but by showing up consistently.

The same principle applies to you. Maybe your efforts aren't immediately recognized, a colleague's emails getting a response or a community organizer's steady events gaining traction. Start small: organize one meeting, send one post online, and let each action speak for itself. The gap between dreaming and doing isn't about the intensity of your passion; it's about how close you get to the work. You can't build confidence from a distance or transform daydreams into a new identity.

True change happens when you move despite the resistance from your inner voices.

> ## "You are not a drop in the ocean. You are the entire ocean in a drop."
>
> — RUMI

I once mentored a woman who dreamed of starting her podcast. She had a name, potential guests, and even a trailer, but she hadn't produced a single episode. Her inner voices were loud: her critic pointed out her amateur sound, her protector urged patience until she had the perfect studio, and her ghost insisted that no one would listen. She could have given up when her first recording failed due to technical issues. Instead, she posted a raw, 10-minute episode. A friend reached out, saying, "I'm stuck too. Thanks for being real." That small, imperfect step built her confidence; one episode led to another, and soon, she had a growing body of work, proof that progress doesn't require perfection.

Your dream, a new garden, a workshop, a small project, faces the same inner resistance. The trick is to act rather than just aspire. Whether it's planting a seed or drafting a slide, taking a single step shifts the dream into reality.

Seeing is believing, but you don't have to wait to be seen. You can start stacking proof right now.

THE FRAMEWORK: **THE PROOF STACK**

Stop admiring from afar and start creating your own proof. The Proof Stack is a system of recording your actions to quiet those inner voices and build self-confidence through small wins. Here's how you build your Proof Stack:

■ **Act Without Permission**

Take one daring step, pitching an idea, posting a draft online, or asking for a role, despite the whisper that you'll fail. For example, email a mentor even if you don't expect an immediate reply.

■ **Log Your Proof**

Write down immediately what you did, how you felt, and the outcome, like "I shared a post, feared judgment, but received likes." This record counters the voice that says your actions are insignificant. Even small wins count.

■ **Reflect on Wins**

Review your log weekly to see that every action is progressing. This reflection quiets the protective inner warning of "Don't risk it." Recognize that every small step builds your credibility.

■ **Build on Momentum**

Stack another small action, such as leaving a comment or leading a project. Momentum compounds, reinforcing your identity as someone who takes action.

Consider everyday scenarios:

■ Learning: "Practiced a new language, feared mistakes, learned a phrase; next, try a conversation."

■ Volunteering: "Helped with a community task, felt awkward, received thanks; next, take on a small leadership role."

■ Family: "Set a new routine, worried about tantrums, achieved it; next, plan a family outing."

■ Creativity: "Painted a canvas, feared critique, got praise; next, share your work in a group."

If your inner critic tries to dismiss your efforts, write down, "This counts." Even if it's a tiny action, it's part of your growing Proof Stack.

Proof Isn't a Personality Trait

It's tempting to believe that some people are just born bold and decisive, while you're wired to hesitate. However, evidence shows that everyone builds what seems like magic through incremental actions. They don't begin with a perfect plan or a grand speech; they start with a clumsy, imperfect step. Over time, these steps accumulate into a foundation of proof: a collection of actions that transform potential into reality.

The day you decide to act, despite your inner doubts, is the day everything changes.

I remember the moment I realized I was the only one who could validate my dreams. It was a rainy Thursday in a coffee shop filled with the scent of burnt espresso and quiet determination. I had spent hours "working on" a project I'd planned out countless times but never started. I was waiting for a magical sign, a deep conviction that would tell me, "Now you are worthy; go ahead." It never came.

Instead, I experienced a profound realization: if I didn't move, nothing would happen. So, I wrote the first clumsy page of what later turned into a full project. I sent that awkward email and posted that imperfect idea online. I stopped waiting for external confirmation and started proving my worth through action. No grand gesture, no viral moment, just a quiet shift from waiting to moving. And every success since then tracks back to that small moment of self-permission.

Change isn't about one genius breakthrough: it's about making the decision to start. It's about choosing to act even when you feel unready, even when your hands shake. It's about building a body of proof so undeniable that even your harshest inner critic must eventually quiet down.

The people you admire didn't suddenly become fearless. They simply grew tired of waiting for the perfect moment. They learned that discomfort is part of growth and that the risk of staying the same is far greater than the risk of trying. You're not lacking courage; you're just lacking proof. And you can build that proof through small, incremental actions.

Proof Over Potential

Let's be clear: potential means nothing unless you turn it into action. It doesn't matter how talented you are if you never show up. It doesn't matter how vivid your dreams are if you never take steps to realize them. One imperfect email, one rough draft, and one shaky conversation are all it takes to start building momentum. That's how habits form, that's how evidence stacks up, and that's how potential becomes real. Don't wait until you're ready; get started now.

You are not special, and that's your superpower. If you feel scared, behind, or unsure, remember that you're not broken, and you're not unique in your struggles. You share the same obstacles and opportunities as the people you admire. They're not special; and neither are you. And that's the best news of all. Because it means you already have everything it takes to get started. The only missing ingredient is your decision to act, to stack those small proofs of progress, one small deliberate step at a time. Today. Not someday, not after you feel "confident." Now.

Remember, proof isn't a personality trait; it's a collection of receipts. Every small action you take is a deposit into your Proof Stack. So, stop waiting for someone else to validate you. Start taking action, and let the evidence speak for itself.

"

YOUR WORST DAY ISN'T THE END OF YOUR JOURNEY; IT'S MERELY A LANDMARK ALONG THE WAY.

"

CHAPTER 12

Pitfalls Are Predictable, Not Permanent

The Myth of Linear Progress

I used to believe that if I worked hard, planned meticulously, and stayed spiritually aligned, my path would be smooth, steady, and straight. I imagined that if you were truly focused and intentional about growing, you wouldn't stumble, lose momentum, or slip back. Progress would simply build on itself like a staircase you only had to climb once. I didn't realize that I was setting myself up for heartache. The moment I hit a real barrier, a true wall, not just a rough patch, I crumbled. I gave that setback too much weight, concluding that it was a judgment of my abilities, a sign that I wasn't made for this or that the very dream I pursued was overly ambitious. In truth, that obstacle was just part of the journey. It wasn't evidence of my failure; it was proof that I was in the process of building something significant.

Why Pitfalls Seem Like Failures (But Are Not)

The real danger isn't in experiencing setbacks; it's in the story you tell yourself when you do. You might miss a workout, fall back into old habits, send a risky email that gets no reply, post something that flops, or bomb an interview. These moments sting because of what occurred and because your inner critic, protector, and even the ghost of past failures start whispering, "See? You're not good enough." With those voices lurking, any misstep feels like confirmation that you shouldn't have dared to try at all.

But here's the truth:

Setbacks don't reflect your worth; they're simply part of the process.

They don't mean you're broken; they mean you're building something real. Every transformational person you admire, from successful entrepreneurs and top athletes to community leaders, you can be sure faced moments that felt like total collapse. They missed opportunities. They embarrassed themselves. They wanted to quit. The crucial distinction is that feeling stuck does not equate to being stuck. You're allowed to fall. You're allowed to have messy chapters. You're allowed to wonder, "How did I end up here?" What matters isn't that you falter but what you do next.

Now that we know setbacks aren't the enemy, let's map the most common ones so you can anticipate them.

Predictable Pitfalls You Will Encounter

There's a harsh kind of mercy in realizing that most setbacks aren't random disasters but predictable patterns rather than punishments. You're not uniquely burdened by hardship. You're simply encountering common milestones that nearly everyone faces on the path to real change. You will experience:

■ The Motivation Crash: That sudden drop in energy once the initial excitement wanes.

■ The Identity Crisis: A period where you've outgrown your old self but haven't fully embraced your new one.

■ The Progress Plateau: A phase where results seem stalled, even though you're still putting in the work.

■ The Comparison Trap: When someone else's highlight reel makes you doubt the value of your own steady progress.

■ The Burnout Bluff: When you overdo it in an attempt to silence your doubts and end up exhausted.

■ The Silent Season: When your hard work goes unnoticed, no applause, no praise, just you and your effort.

If you haven't heard it before, listen well: **Progress isn't a straight line.** It's a messy, winding, and jagged path punctuated with setbacks, low points, pauses, doubts, and hard days. These challenges aren't failures; they're simply markers that you're alive. Growth doesn't happen in a perfect bubble, it happens amid life's friction. When you bump into a wall, it doesn't mean you're doing something wrong; it means you're moving forward.

None of these indicate that you're on the wrong path. They're evidence that you're engaging in the messy, unseen, and essential part of growth that many never witness and quite a few give up on entirely. This chapter isn't about pretending these setbacks won't hurt, they do, but it's about recognizing them so you can respond with strategy rather than succumb to shame. You won't be thrown off course by a setback you expected; you'll steady yourself, adjust, and climb back up.

The Setback Recovery Loop

Many believe that bouncing back from a setback is about "getting back to normal." It isn't. If you aim merely to return to your previous state, you miss the valuable insight a setback provides. The goal isn't to rewind; it's to rebound. When you comprehend this, you stop rushing to erase a bad day and begin to mine it for lessons.

Here's how it unfolds:

You hit a wall, emotional, logistical, or sheer exhaustion, and fall short. Immediately, your mind starts assigning meaning: "I'm lazy," "I'm not cut out for this," and "This proves I'm not good enough." At this fork, you can either spiral into shame, reinforcing a negative identity that makes future efforts harder or spiral into strategy, studying the wall, asking the right questions like, "What system failed?" "What support was missing?" "What expectations were unrealistic?" "How can I reframe this next time?" True recovery isn't about pretending the fall didn't happen; it's about extracting wisdom from it and moving forward more intelligently, not just with more force.

I didn't learn this overnight. There was a time when every missed goal plunged me into a spiral of shame. Miss a writing deadline? I'd abandon writing for weeks. Skip a fitness class? I convinced myself that exercise wasn't for me. Each small failure became a massive indictment, confirming my deepest fears and urging me to play even smaller. Until one day, after yet another missed opportunity, I sat with my journal, tired of repeating the same self-loathing narrative. I asked, almost defiantly, "What if this isn't proof that I'm broken, but just evidence that I'm building?" That small break in my narrative let in a ray of light. Perhaps these missteps weren't signs of inadequacy but evidence of engagement and proof that I was trying, something many never dare to do. That realization didn't make the falls hurt any less, but it made me determined to move forward with each fall, not backward.

If knowing the loop is step one, step two is architecting your comeback before you ever need it.

How to Pre-Plan Your Comeback

Since reaching a low point is inevitable, why not prepare beforehand? Don't wait until you're hurting to find the bandages. Prepare your comeback while your mind is clear and your spirit is steady.

Here's what that looks like:

1. Choose Your Bounce-Back Phrase

When you fall, your mind will naturally grab the easiest narrative. If you don't provide one intentionally, your inner critic will supply it. Choose a short, powerful phrase you can use immediately; something like, "This is a data point, not a death sentence," "I build resilience, not perfection," or "Falling means I'm moving." Mine is: "This is just the next part of the story." Simple, true, and enough.

2. Identify Your Signal Action

When you feel overwhelmed and drained of energy, you need one clear, non-negotiable action to break that cycle. A "signal action" signals your nervous system that you're still in motion. It might be writing one paragraph, moving for five minutes, sending a quick text, or logging a tiny piece of proof. It's not about conquering the day; it's about refusing to let the fall define it. That first small move is transformative because even a tiny action can shatter the paralysis of shame.

3. Set a Recovery Window

Don't let a bad moment stretch into a bad month. Pre-determine how long you'll allow yourself to grieve, falter, and then re-engage: 24 hours, three days, or even one week at most. Without a limit, your mind might default to endless delay, letting pain fester. Clear boundaries interrupt that cycle.

A QUICK STORY: **THE 24HOUR RECOVERY RULE**

When I started writing publicly, rejection would shatter me. A declined pitch, a silent post, or a harsh review could send me into weeks of inertia. Eventually, I established a rule: 24 hours of permission. If something hurt, I allowed myself those 24 hours to grieve fully, whether that meant crying, ranting, journaling, eating ice cream, or simply hunkering down without judgment. But once that period ended, I had to take action, not because I suddenly felt ready, but because the rule demanded it. At first, it felt forced and mechanical, but it became my lifeline after several cycles. I learned that even reluctant motion is far more healing than endless self-pity. Today, I continue to honor the 24-hour rule because setbacks are a given, but staying stuck is a choice.

No guilt. No pressure to "fix" anything.

- **Hour 0–6:** Feel it. Cry, rant, journal, whatever helps you unload.

- **Hour 6–12:** Rest. Step away: go for a walk, sleep, or do something restorative.

- **Hour 12–18:** Reflect. Ask, "What can I learn?" and jot down any insights.

▪ **Hour 18–24:** Act. Choose one tiny "signal action" (write one sentence, send one email, take a fiveminute walk) and do it before the clock strikes 24.

Why 24 hours? Because shorter windows deny you real closure; longer windows let shame fester. One day gives just enough space to honor your feelings, and then forces momentum before selfpity becomes routine.

What's Coming Next

You aren't broken because you struggle or lagging because you fall. You're not unworthy simply because you waver. You are on a journey, and that journey is intentionally messy. In our next phase, we'll build your personal Setback Recovery System: a tailored protocol for those moments when motivation crashes, doubt creeps in, or life throws you off balance. You don't have to fear the fall; you need to train for the rise.

Building Your Setback Recovery System

Imagine constructing a skyscraper. You wouldn't wait for an earthquake to design your reinforcements. Instead, you'd build anticipating the shakes, ensuring the structure could flex without collapsing. That's how you should view your life. Not if storms occur but when they inevitably do. When they do, you won't "rise by magic." You'll fall to the level of your preparation. That's why you need a Setback Recovery System: a simple, intentional plan to catch you before you spiral. It needn't be overly complicated or overwhelming; it just needs to be robust enough to support you when all you feel is the urge to quit.

Step 1: Pre-Write Your Bounce-Back Script

Don't wait until you're emotionally shattered to figure out what to say to yourself. Write your script now. In moments of failure, your brain defaults to the easiest narrative, often a negative one. You need to over-write that with a positive, empowering routine. Write a short script you can recite when you fall, such as: "I am not broken. I am building. This setback is only a scene, not the whole story. I move forward now, not because it's easy, but because I can." Keep it short, potent, and close by. It could be on your phone, desk, or mirror so your future self can borrow strength from your words.

Step 2: Define Your Non-Negotiable Action

Action annihilates shame. It doesn't have to be grand; it just has to be genuine. Commit to one tiny action even when you feel completely overwhelmed. Maybe it's writing one sentence, moving for three minutes, reaching out to a friend, or simply opening your planner even when you don't feel like it. This isn't about productivity; it's about proof that you can still take steps forward, regardless of how little motivation remains. The size of the action doesn't matter; what matters is that you follow through.

Step 3: Set Your Recovery Timeline

Shame thrives on ambiguity. The longer you allow yourself to linger without a clear schedule, the deeper you'll sink. Decide in advance: when you fall, and you will, how long will you let yourself grieve before re-engaging? Put a boundary around it, whether it's one day, three days, or a week. Without limits, negative thoughts can spiral indefinitely. Structuring your recovery time disrupts that process.

Step 4: Ritualize Your Reflection

Many either dwell on their mistakes or force through them without gleaning lessons. Neither method builds resilience. You need to reflect from a place of strategy, not judgment. Create a simple ritual after setbacks by asking yourself: What triggered this fall? Which system or support was missing? What can I adjust for next time? Avoid questions like "What's wrong with me?" Instead, focus on what broke and how you can strengthen it.

Real Life: The Pivot That Saved My Career

There was a time when everything seemed to collapse simultaneously: a failed product launch, a relationship ending, and unfulfilled commitments I was too embarrassed to admit I couldn't handle. The version of me that believed in simply "muscling through" was shattered. I remember sitting in a coffee shop with my laptop open but nothing to write, my heart racing as shame engulfed me. I ignored the warning signs and the growing cracks for months, insisting that hard work would fix everything. But hustle only masks structural flaws, never mending them. That day, I grabbed a blank notebook and, instead of listing tasks, wrote, "My success isn't measured by never falling; it's measured by creating better ways to stand back up." That one page was the seed from which my Setback Recovery System grew. It wasn't dramatic or glamorous; it was simply real. One decision redirected everything.

The Science of Bouncing Back

Psychologists call it "psychological flexibility," your ability to adapt when life doesn't go as planned. Studies show that this flexibility predicts long-term success far better than IQ, talent, or grit. It's not about avoiding falls but how you respond when they occur. And that response is built now, not later when you're already in a spiral. By crafting your script, defining your action, setting a timeline, and ritualizing your reflection, you create resilience, not just surviving storms but using them to rebuild yourself stronger than before.

REFLECTION PROMPT: **YOUR RECOVERY BLUEPRINT**

Pause and write this down:

My Bounce-Back Script: "When I fall, I will tell myself:

"

My Signal Action: "When I feel stuck, I will:

"

My Recovery Window: "I give myself

to grieve before taking action."

My Reflection Ritual: "After setbacks, I will ask: (1) What triggered this? (2) What was missing? (3) What can I adjust?"

Underline it, highlight it, and own it. You're no longer waiting for perfection but positioning yourself to rise faster.

Understand this: you're going to fall. Not just once or twice, but many times. Some days will leave you feeling devastated, some failures will sting, and some missteps will urge you to hide away. But the difference between those who build lives they're proud of and those who remain stuck isn't the number of times they fall but the number of times they recover. The people you admire aren't immune to failure; they simply refuse to stay down. And now, neither will you. Not because you'll never fall again but because you won't let a fall define your story. You are not fragile. You are not broken. You are in motion, constantly evolving into an anti-fragile version of yourself, one bounce-back at a time.

ACTION PROMPT: **BOUNCE BACK WITHIN 72 HOURS**

Here's your first field test:

The next time you experience a setback, because it will happen, your mission is to recover within 72 hours. Not to achieve perfection, fix every problem, or wait until you feel completely ready, but simply to take one step forward. Even if it's small or feels trivial or awkward, that action disrupts the cycle of shame. It sends a message to your brain: "Falling isn't fatal; movement is always an option." By acting quickly, you condition yourself to bounce back rather than letting failure cement itself into your identity.

For example, I ran a campaign I'd poured months into a few years ago, only to face silence on launch day. Old me would have spiraled into self-doubt, hidden under the weight of failure for weeks. This time, I used my system: I granted myself 24 hours to process the disappointment, then took action by posting an honest reflection about what didn't work and what I learned. That small act closed the loop of shame and reminded me that I still had a voice and momentum. The 72-hour rule saved me then, and it can save you, too.

Common Setback Scripts You Need to Break

If you want to master bouncing back, recognize the common narratives that your mind might try to enforce:

"This always happens to me."

"See? I wasn't cut out for this."

"It's too late now. What's the point?"

"Everyone saw me fail, I'll never recover."

These aren't rational assessments but emotional reflexes, echoes from your critic, protector, and ghost trying to hold you back. You don't need to debate them; you simply need to counter them with proof that you can still act, rebuild, and move forward, even if progress is slow, messy, and uncertain.

Shift From Fragile to Anti-Fragile

In nature, some things shatter under pressure while others endure. The rarest, however, are those that actually grow stronger. They're called anti-fragile. You're training to become one of those: a person who doesn't just survive storms by luck or brute force but transforms pressure into fuel. Every time you bounce back, you're not just returning to where you were; you're building thicker skin, honing your vision, and deepening your belief in yourself. Your goal isn't to avoid stress but to grow robust enough that stress refines you rather than defines you. This quiet shift is the superpower behind every person you admire. They aren't unshaken because they are invincible. They're unshaken because they expect to be shaken and trust themselves to rebound.

REFLECTION PROMPT: **YOUR ANTIFRAGILE BLUEPRINT**

Take a moment to jot this down:

When I fall, I will tell myself:

" _____ "

When I feel ashamed, my first action will be:

" _____ "

When setbacks occur, I commit to recovering within:

" _____ hours."

My proof that I'm becoming anti-fragile is:

" _____ "

Keep this blueprint somewhere you can see it daily and return to it after every fall to reinforce your resilience.

Let's keep it real. Everyone loves to celebrate success, the break-throughs, and the highlight reels. But real, lasting strength is forged in the aftermath of crashes when applause fades, and you rebuild when no one's watching. Success doesn't just reward effort, it rewards recovery. It honors those willing to be vulnerable, underestimated, and even messy yet choose to keep moving. The door you're striving to enter doesn't demand fearless perfection; it asks for willingness: willingness to fall, to try again, and to trade ego for endurance. Remember, those who seem "ahead" are simply the ones who have mastered the art of getting back up. And now you will too, not because you'll never stumble, but because you refuse to let any fall become your final chapter.

YOU ARE NOT
FRAGILE.

YOU ARE NOT
BROKEN.

YOU ARE IN MOTION,
CONTINUOUSLY GROWING
INTO AN ANTI-
FRAGILE VERSION
OF YOURSELF,
ONE BOUNCE-BACK
AT A TIME.

LET'S KEEP MOVING
FORWARD.

05

PART FIVE

NEVER LOOK BACK

"

YOUR MIND IS
EITHER A TOOL YOU
WIELD WISELY OR A
BATTLEGROUND WHERE
YOU CONTINUALLY
FACE DEFEAT, AS
ECHOED IN THE WORDS
OF MAHATMA GANDHI,
"THE ENEMY IS FEAR.
WE THINK IT IS HATE,
BUT IT IS FEAR."

"

CHAPTER 13

Bulletproof Your Mind

Why Mindset Is More Than a Catchphrase, It's the Engine of Your Life

These days, you hear the word "mindset" everywhere. It's splashed on posters, printed on journals, and tagged under motivational quotes. With such overuse, it's easy to brush it off with a casual "Yeah, I know what mindset is." But here's a fact you can't ignore: mindset isn't just a pretty word; it's about survival. It's not decorative or just empty motivation on your wall. It's the very system that governs how you interpret everything and how you view challenges, understand failure, and react to pressure, tiredness, boredom, or success. Your way of thinking can be the force behind exponential growth or the root of repeated setbacks, turning obstacles into stepping stones or barriers that hold you back. Whether you know it or not, your mindset is always at work. The issue isn't its existence but whether it's resilient or fragile.

The Three Mindsets That Undermine Your Progress

Before diving into how to create an unyielding mind, let's expose the subtle mental habits that sap your potential. You might even catch yourself grappling with one of these rights now.

1. The Fragile Mindset: "If it's hard, it's wrong."

This perspective equates difficulty with a signal to back away. Whether it's an uncomfortable new job, a slow start to a business, or the painful growth process, this mindset assumes that ease is the norm and buckles when met with pressure.

2. The Victim Mindset: "Things happen to me, not because of me."

At times, blaming bad luck, unsympathetic bosses, or missed opportunities may seem reasonable. However, over time, this mentality robs you of control, making you a passive actor in your story while convincing you that change lies only in external forces rather than within yourself.

3. The All-or-Nothing Mindset: "If it's not perfect, it's pointless."

This way of thinking demands grand gestures. It declares that if you can't commit 100 percent, there's no point in trying at all. One missed day and the streak is ruined; a small misstep and the whole effort feels worthless. This mindset often leads people to give up on even brilliant ideas because of minor setbacks.

So what? Spotting these traps is the first step, now let's learn how to dissolve them.

A Story of Nearly Giving Up

There was a night a couple of years ago when I almost abandoned everything I'd built. I had poured months of preparation into a new project: late nights, personal savings, and sharing my vision with loved ones, only to be met with silence, low engagement, and disappointing sales. Alone at my desk, I began filling out job applications as my inner voices whispered doubts: the Critic lamented my embarrassment, the Protector urged safety, and the Ghost insisted I wasn't meant for this. I wasn't seeking drama or pity, I truly questioned my potential. Then I rediscovered a sticky note I'd written months earlier: "The work works if you work it." That simple message cut through the noise, reminding me that success isn't about instant results but staying the course. That night, I took a small step and sent a new email to my list, which didn't perform well either, but it kept me in the game. Six weeks later, after many days of unseen efforts, that persistence led to a partnership that changed everything, not because I was extraordinary, but because I refused to let a fragile mindset win.

"The work works
if you work it."

— MY MIDNIGHT REMINDER WHEN I ALMOST QUIT

Developing a Resilient, Bulletproof Mindset

Building a bulletproof mindset isn't about arrogance or feigning a lack of fear, frustration, or exhaustion. It's about cultivating inner habits that propel you forward, even when overwhelming emotions overwhelm you. It means learning to see resistance not as a condemnation but as an invitation, setbacks as data rather than defeat, and effort as proof of progress rather than a sign of failure. It's about realizing that life isn't assessing your raw talent but testing your relationship with struggle. The people you admire didn't avoid hardship; they transformed it into fuel rather than allowing it to dampen their spirits. This is the genuine work of transforming your mind: not motivational catchphrases, but real rewiring, resilience, and momentum.

How a Resilient Mind Approaches Challenges

Consider this simple breakdown:

■ When obstacles arise, a fragile mindset might think, "This shouldn't happen," whereas a resilient mindset responds, "This is bound to happen; let's adapt."

■ Faced with failure, a fragile mind might hide in embarrassment, while a resilient mind recognizes its humanity and extracts lessons.

■ When fear roars, a fragile mind waits for courage, but a resilient mind understands that action is possible even amidst fear.

The difference is subtle and internal, yet it fundamentally alters your trajectory.

REFLECTION PROMPT: **CULTIVATE YOUR ANTI-FRAGILE MINDSET**

Take a moment, don't just read this; act on it. Ask yourself:

■ What current obstacle seems insurmountable?

....

....

■ Which three inner voices (the Critic, Protector, and Ghost) are loudest when you face them?

....

....

■ How would a resilient, bulletproof mind respond to each?

....

....

■ What is one small action you can take today to shift from a fragile to an anti-fragile mindset?

....

....

Write down your answers and place them somewhere visible. Remember, your mindset isn't something you just possess; it's something you continuously build, one brick at a time.

When My Inner Critic Nearly Overpowered Me

There was a week when I had to present a major proposal to an executive team, a high-stakes opportunity I'd prepared for over several days. On the morning of the presentation, however, my inner Critic was relentless: "You'll sound unprepared. They'll ask questions you can't answer. They'll see you don't belong here." I felt the anxiety in my chest, the nervous tremor during practice runs, and even considered calling in sick. Yet, something I had trained myself to do kicked in: I acknowledged my fear instead of trying to eliminate it. Then I asked myself, "What would a confident person do, even if they didn't feel confident yet?" The answer was clear: they'd show up, walk into the room, and deliver what they'd prepared. So I did just that. I wasn't filled with bravery or certainty, but I carried out my plan, and the presentation went well, not flawlessly, but solid enough to spark follow-up interest. That day didn't turn me fearless, but it reinforced that you don't have to feel invincible to act like it. Every small step builds your mental muscle.

Having seen how mental muscle works in practice, let's build your own gym:

The 3-Second Rule for Reframing Your Thoughts

Shifting your mindset doesn't require lengthy meditations or extended retreats. Sometimes, all it takes is three seconds to catch a negative spiral and alter your reaction.

Step 1: Notice the Negative Thought

When a defeatist notion pops up "I can't do this," "This always happens to me," or "What's the point?" pause momentarily. Instead of fighting it, simply acknowledge its presence.

Step 2: Ask Yourself a Simple Question

"What's another way to view this moment?" This question doesn't force a lie; it opens your mind to a different perspective. Instead of interpreting failure as proof of inadequacy, consider it useful feedback on where to improve. Instead of feeling rejected because someone didn't respond, remind yourself that they're busy and your worth isn't defined by an isolated moment. This is a mindset rep, and with enough practice, it will become second nature.

So what? Three seconds is all it takes to interrupt a spiral, so practice the pause.

The "Prove-It" Practice

If you want to rewire your belief system, start actively proving positive things to yourself, even through small, consistent actions. I call this the "Prove-It" Practice, which is an effective way to build mental armor. Choose a belief you want to embody, for example, "I finish what I start." Then, identify a micro-action that reinforces this belief, like writing for five minutes, doing one push-up, or completing a small task. Track each instance not as an obsession but to build a bank of evidence that substantiates your new identity. I did this with my writing, logging even a few hundred words daily. It may have seemed trivial at first, but consistency transformed my mindset over time.

Think of your mindset like a muscle: it only grows when you give it repeated, targeted reps, flashy oneoffs won't cut it. Every 3second reframe, every tiny 'ProveIt' action you log, is a mental repetition that carves clearer neural pathways and strengthens your inner resilience.

The Mindset Field Kit

Below are some practical strategies I've used and taught to bolster mental resilience:

1. The "Failure Folder"

Keep a folder (digital or physical) filled with examples of things that didn't go as planned: rejected pitches, missed opportunities, or unproductive emails. Label it as "Evidence I Survived." Review it monthly, and you'll realize you're still standing, you've overcome before, and that failure loses its sting once you accept it.

2. The Win Vault

We often dwell on mistakes, but do you consistently document your successes? Start a "Win Vault" where you capture moments when your work was appreciated, screenshots of positive comments, or instances where you felt proud, even if quietly. On tough days, these reminders become your shield.

3. The Identity Anchor

Craft a concise statement that encapsulates who you're striving to be: "I remain calm under pressure," "I'm a builder who finishes what I start," or "I make my vision a reality." Recite this before important decisions, when your inner Critic starts to chatter, or when fear arises. Repeat it until it feels ingrained in you.

PAUSE AND CREATE YOUR REWIRING RITUAL

Bring this theory into practice. Today, design a personal Rewiring Ritual by answering these prompts:

- One mindset I want to shift is:

"   "
....

- One belief I want to install is:

"   "
....

- One small action that supports that belief is:

"   "
....

- I'll track that action in: [Notion / notebook / voice memos]

....

- My new identity anchor is:

"   "
....

Write it down, speak it aloud, and practice it repeatedly. Repetition is the only tool that truly rewires your brain.

Why Mindset Isn't the Same as Motivation (And What to Build Instead)

If you think making your mind bulletproof is about feeling inspired all the time, think again. Motivation is fleeting, a mood that fluctuates like the weather. In contrast, your mindset is a robust system, the infrastructure that keeps you moving forward when your initial burst of inspiration fades. You've likely experienced how a motivational video or quote can spark energy for only a few hours or a day at most. While motivation has its power, it's unreliable. Basing your entire life over- haul on "feeling ready" sets you up for predictable disappointment. Instead, focus on building mental infrastructure through routines that aren't swayed by emotion, rituals that firmly anchor your identity and systems that carry you through moments when your willpower wanes.

Ultimately, mindset is less about feelings and more about your decisive actions when those feelings falter.

The Day I Didn't Feel Like It (But Did It Anyway)

There was a morning when I was overwhelmed by deadlines, exhaus- tion, a cluttered inbox, and zero inspiration, when every fiber of my being wanted to give up. I stared at my calendar, hoping the writing block would vanish, looked at a blank document for answers, and even sipped coffee, hoping for a miracle. Meanwhile, my inner voices chimed in: the Critic said, "You're off your game today," the Ghost whispered, "Skip it; no one will notice," and the Protector warned me about burning out if I pushed too hard. Despite their constant urging, I recalled the identity I aimed to build: "I'm someone who writes no matter what." So I allowed myself to write poorly, not perfectly or pro- lifically, just enough to keep going. I ended up typing 127 words that weren't my best work, but I recorded that I showed up even when I didn't feel like it. That small act didn't transform everything overnight, but it kept the momentum alive. Because progress doesn't require per- fection; it just needs consistency.

Emotional Endurance Over Instant Breakthroughs

One of the most undervalued aspects of mental strength is emotional endurance. It isn't about dodging discomfort altogether but about persisting through it. This endurance keeps you applying for opportunities even when you're ghosted, creating content despite a lack of response, and building your vision when applause seems absent. It's neither glamorous nor immediately gratifying; it's gritty, slow, and often goes unnoticed. Yet, it's the very quality that differentiates dabblers from true builders. The good news is that you can train your nervous system to understand that tension isn't dangerous, silence isn't equivalent to failure, and rejection doesn't define you. I practice this by recognizing the moment of discomfort and acknowledging when I want to quit, when I feel unworthy, or when I want to withdraw, and then committing to take just one more small step. That's how resilience is built: not by avoiding faltering moments but by refusing to quit entirely during them.

The Danger of Identity Fragility

Let's address a truth that many won't admit: too many of us base our sense of self on outcomes rather than the effort we put in. We think, "I'm a leader if people follow me," "I'm a writer if I get published," or "I'm successful if I receive validation." But when the desired outcome doesn't materialize, you begin to doubt the project and yourself. This is identity fragility. It causes you to unravel when things don't go as planned. The antidote is to anchor your identity in the process rather than in external praise. You become a writer the moment you start writing, a leader the moment you serve, and a builder the moment you begin. Over time, results may follow, but your core identity is built right now through your consistent efforts.

Reframing Failure with the Identity Dashboard

Here's an effective tool I share with coaching clients when they hit a wall. It's called the Identity Dashboard, a simple, private exercise that helps you reframe failures and adjust your mindset. Create a table with these four columns: ·

- What happened

- What it meant to me

- A better interpretation

- What I'll do next

For example:

- "No one replied to my pitch" could become "I'm not ready," which you can reframe as "Everyone is busy, and taking that step was brave," and then plan to "Follow up or pitch someone else."

- A failed post might transform from "I'm not interesting" to "Algorithms aren't the measure of my worth," leading to a plan to "Post again next week."

By articulating these shifts on paper, you reclaim control over your narrative, stopping the spiral and taking charge.

Preventing Burnout in Your Mental State

Simply put, a resilient mindset doesn't mean you never break down; it means you know how to recover when you do. Burnout-proofing your mind isn't about avoiding stress entirely; it's about designing recovery habits that keep you functional under pressure. For instance, create a default decompression tactic: a specific action, like taking a walk, practicing breathwork, or spending ten minutes in silence, to signal that you're winding down. Develop a "pause phrase," a mantra like, "I've weathered this before, and I can again," to use in moments of overwhelm. Log these restorative moments as you would a workout rep because rest, just like effort, is essential. Remember, burnout usually comes not from doing too much but from doing too much without enough recovery. A truly resilient mindset knows when to advance and when to pull back.

Before Wrapping Up

Pause and reflect for a moment. What if your strongest mindset wasn't defined by constant feelings of strength but by showing up even when you didn't feel strong? What if true confidence wasn't about loud declarations but a quiet inner voice urging, "Let's try again tomorrow"? That is what being bulletproof is all about, not an absence of pain, but an ability to keep going, no matter what. The world isn't asking for a polished version of you; it needs you, messy and determined, the one who endures and builds the life you're destined for.

Your Mindset Operating System

By now, you likely have systems that accumulate evidence of your progress and habits that vote for the person you're becoming. But mindset? It's the operating system that not only drives your behavior but also interprets every experience. Without a resilient mindset, victories might feel insignificant, and setbacks can spiral out of control. So what's the solution? Upgrade your mental operating system. Stop worrying about failure and start asking, "What if I'm becoming someone who handles it all?" Shift your focus from waiting to feel certain to building certainty through consistent rhythm instead of fleeting emotion. Because while emotions can deceive, steady habits and routine prove your worth.

BUILDING YOUR MINDSET BASELINE: **A TACTICAL EXERCISE**

Get practical now. This isn't just a feel-good journaling prompt; it's a calibration tool for your inner system. Create a table (in your notes or journal) with these columns:

TRIGGER	*"No one liked my post"*
OLD THOUGHT	*"I'm not interesting"*
UPGRADED THOUGHT	*"This post is just one rep; my message will evolve."*
ACTION	*"Post again next week."*

Each time you engage in this exercise, you're actively rewiring your brain's response to challenges, not ignoring pain but learning to see discomfort as information rather than danger.

REFLECTION PROMPT: **YOUR RESILIENCE RESET**

As we close, take a moment to write down your reset:

■   What recurring thought do you revert to when you're spiraling?

....

....

■   What action always pulls you back up?

....

....

■   What belief do you want to anchor, even when life tests you?

....

....

Then complete this sentence:

"The version of me I'm becoming doesn't _____.
They _____ instead."

For example:

"The version of me I'm becoming doesn't shut down when things go quiet. They remain steady and keep building."

Today, train your mind as you would your body, one rep, one pause, one proof at a time, and watch your resilience become truly bulletproof.

Final Takeaway: Mindset Over Motivation

You don't need a magically "stronger" mind; you need one that's been trained through practice, a mindset forged in honest reflection, consistent action, and deliberate repetition. There's no off switch, only a system you refine over time. The more you engage that system, the more unshakeable you become. Remember, it's not about perfection or constant intensity; it's about quiet, consistent commitment. Keep your promises, log your progress, and reframe your setbacks. Eventually, your mind won't react with bluster. It will settle into a calm, steady force that endures every challenge.

And when all is said and done, it won't be about always feeling invincible. It'll be about being the person who, no matter what, keeps showing up, and that is truly bulletproof.

"IT'S NOT ABOUT ALWAYS FEELING INVINCIBLE. IT'S ABOUT SHOWING UP ANYWAY, AND THAT IS TRULY BULLETPROOF."

- CHAPTER 13 CLOSING MANTRA

ACCOUNTABILITY BREEDS RESPONSE-ABILITY.

— STEPHEN R. COVEY

CHAPTER 14

Accountability: A Must-Have

"The price of greatness is responsibility."

– WINSTON CHURCHILL

Why Relying Solely on Willpower Won't Cut It

If you're still trying to force your way through progress with sheer will-power, let's face it: that method is bound to let you down. It's not a matter of weakness but simply part of being human. Studies, like Dr. Roy Baumeister's research on ego depletion, reveal that willpower functions like a battery: it slowly drains with every decision you make, every temptation you resist, and every new task you take on. The same goes for motivation; it ebbs and flows with your mood, sleep, stress, and even the weather. This means that if your entire strategy for success is to "be stronger next time," you are setting yourself up for disappointment. You don't thrive because of your good intentions. You succeed because of the infrastructure you build around them. And the strongest foundation for long-term change? Accountability.

The Unseen Strength of Being Observed

I first discovered this lesson while preparing to launch my inaugural online course. I had everything ready, the content was polished and the audience was waiting. Yet, every day, I found a new reason to postpone it.

"I'm perfecting the curriculum," I convinced myself. "I'm enhancing the student experience." In reality, I was just hiding behind excuses.

Then, one evening, during a casual group chat with a few trusted colleagues, someone asked, "So, when's your course dropping?"

I mumbled something tentative about it coming "soon" and being "in alignment."

That's when one of them remarked, "We're all launching by the end of next month, right?" That statement felt like a clear boundary, a mirror reflecting my inaction.

I felt cornered. Strangely enough, I was relieved because, suddenly, it wasn't just a private promise I could easily break. It became public. Witnessed. Named.

Almost magically, my behavior changed. Not because my willpower suddenly increased but because my surroundings made it impossible not to act.

Accountability Isn't About Policing

This isn't about feeling ashamed or having someone hovering over you.

True accountability is not like a strict cop; it's more like a dependable mirror. It doesn't scold; it simply reflects.

It holds you accountable to your highest intentions when your worst habits try to take over.

Think about having a workout partner. You don't show up out of fear of being yelled at; you show up because you made a commitment, and you know they're counting on you.

That's the essence of effective accountability: it's not about pressure but partnership.

It reminds you of the person you promised to become, especially on those days when you almost forget.

Why We Shy Away From Accountability

If accountability is so valuable, then why do we often resist it? The answer is simple: it challenges the part of us that desperately clings to an escape route. Without external accountability, you can always find room to say, "I'm still working on it." "I just need a bit more time." "I'm not ready yet." But once you invite someone else to be part of your journey, time begins to work differently. Uncertainty loses its grip. Excuses sound empty. The silence becomes deafening. There's no hiding behind "almost" anymore. Either you move forward or you don't. For many, this exposure is intimidating. There's nowhere to hide when someone sees you trying and possibly failing.

Yet here lies the paradox:

Being seen doesn't reveal your shortcomings but unlocks your inner strength.

It shows you that progress is more important than pride and that showing up, even imperfectly, is far better than remaining stagnant.

The Promise That Gave Life to This Book

When I began writing this book, I had every excuse in the book to delay it. There's a vulnerability in exposing the truths you once hid from yourself. It's even tougher without a looming deadline or external push. I knew I could easily justify postponing:

"I'll write when inspiration strikes." "I'll launch when everything is perfect." So, before I penned a single word, I told a few trusted individuals, "I'm writing this book, and it will be finished by [specific date]." I didn't send them drafts or ask for feedback. I merely gave them the freedom to ask one simple question every week: "How's the writing going?" That uninterrupted thread of accountability carried me through the difficult days when a little voice whispered, "No one will care," or when my inner critic suggested, "Maybe you should scrap the whole idea." It wasn't the pressure that propelled me; it was the constant reminder that I had made a choice and that these people believed in me.

REFLECTION PROMPT: **WHO WILL HOLD YOUR AMBITION?**

Think of one goal you've been quietly pursuing or even avoiding. Ask yourself: Who would you trust to hold your ambition space without judgment? What is the simplest, most straightforward promise you could make to them?

For example:

"I'll send one rough draft each month."

"I'll record my daily progress in a shared document."

"I'll check in every Friday to share my small wins."

Keep it simple, specific, and shared.

Accountability Isn't a Crutch, It's a Catalyst

We sometimes deceive ourselves with the notion:

"If I were truly committed, I wouldn't need accountability."

That's simply not true.

Top athletes have coaches. World-class performers practice with partners. CEOs rely on boards and advisors.

Accountability isn't a sign of weakness; it's the structure that turns good intentions into tangible progress.

It ensures your goals remain larger than temporary feelings.

When you know someone will ask, "Did you do what you promised?" your mindset shifts. Procrastination diminishes, excuses become laughable, and action seems more attainable.

It isn't about impressing anyone but remaining true to the person you vowed to become.

The Problem with Internal Promises

Here's a hard truth: Most promises we make to ourselves are easy to renegotiate. We say, "I'll work out tomorrow." We say, "I'll send that pitch next week." Then tomorrow arrives, and nothing happens. Next week comes, and the goal moves further away.

Sunday comes, and we find a soft excuse: "I was tired." "I wasn't ready." "I'll be better next month." These excuses may feel comforting and reasonable, but they slowly erode trust, not in others but in yourself.

Every broken promise, even the small ones, chips away at your belief in your own words. It trains your mind to see your intentions as mere suggestions rather than solid commitments. And before you know it, you start doubting yourself. That's the hidden cost of going it alone. What feels like giving yourself grace often becomes an easy escape from the discomfort that fuels growth.

When No One Is Watching

The Hawthorne Effect, well-documented in industrial research, shows that people adjust their behavior simply because they know they're being observed. It isn't about feeling pressured or ashamed; it's about the power of being present. Just knowing that someone is watching, even passively, sharpens your commitment. You've likely experienced it: you work harder when the boss passes by, sit up straighter when someone glances your way, and double-check your emails when you know they'll be reviewed. Even one person watching can bring out a more focused, stronger version of yourself. Now, imagine using that principle on purpose, not just by chance.

Imagine creating a small circle where your achievements, setbacks, and promises aren't private dreams but public agreements, not in a judgmental way, but in a way that honors your future. That is the true power of accountability, visibility that brings honor and drives momentum.

The Accountability Gap

Many people fall into a dangerous middle ground: They make bold announcements (New Year's resolutions, public declarations), yet they lack a personal framework to follow through. They have a crowd but lack genuine connection. They have followers but not the friction needed for real growth. Sharing your goals on social media might feel exhilarating, but it provides only superficial accountability. No one is truly monitoring your progress, fully aware of your milestones, or emotionally invested in your journey. That's why an external audience alone isn't enough. You need someone or a small circle of trusted individuals who know exactly what you promised. People who notice when you falter and gently remind you of the person you vowed to become. Without that intimate support, even the best intentions can wither under life's distractions.

Building True Accountability

If you're truly committed to change, you need a system that renders excuses irrelevant. Not one that's harsh, but one that's intimate, focused, and genuine.

Here's what that system might look like:

1. Keep It Intimate

Large groups rarely foster deep accountability. Three committed partners can transform your progress far more than a crowd of hundreds.

Choose accountability partners who meet three criteria:

- Commitment: They're genuinely invested in their growth.

- Candor: They're willing to speak the truth without sugarcoating it for your comfort.

- Compassion: They support you firmly without enabling your excuses.

Even one person is valuable; two are excellent, and a trio is ideal. Beyond that, the intimacy tends to dissolve, and people start hiding behind each other. Remember, accountability isn't about performing for an audience. It's about becoming sharper through close, honest connections.

2. Make Specific Promises

General promises crumble under pressure. Saying, "I'll be healthier," "I'll work on my business," or "I'll put myself out there" lacks the detail you need.

Specific commitments save you.

For instance:

"I will send one pitch email by Friday at 3 PM."

"I will record and post one unedited video by Thursday."

"I will walk 7,000 steps daily for the next five days."

Clear promises lead to clear evidence, whereas vague commitments only breed vague guilt.

3. Schedule Regular Check-Ins

Don't wait for the perfect moment to review your progress; make the check-ins automatic.

Whether it's a five-minute call, a weekly voice note, or a Sunday text thread asking, "What did you ship this week?" the key is consistency.

It doesn't have to feel heavy; it just has to be real.

Regular rhythm turns your intentions into reality. Without scheduled touchpoints, even the most determined goals can drift away.

4. Celebrate Progress, Not Perfection

Accountability shouldn't feel like being on trial.

It isn't about setting up a judgmental tribunal to highlight your mistakes. It's about keeping a steady flame alive when your motivation wanes.

Focus on acknowledging what you've accomplished, even if it's imperfect:

"You delivered a rough version, amazing job."

"You sought feedback, even when it was uncomfortable, huge step."

"You showed up on a day you really didn't want to, truly inspiring."

Remember: it's about progress, not performance; movement, not medals.

That's how momentum carries you through tough days and weeks, moving you steadily forward.

Becoming Someone You Can Count On

The true magic of accountability isn't about what you prove to others but what you prove to yourself. Every time you show up, even if it's messy; every time you deliver, even if it's late; every time you admit a mistake but recommit, you're reshaping your self-image. You stop being someone who merely hopes to follow through and become someone who expects to keep their word. This transformation starts subtly, almost unseen by others, but inside, it's transformative.

When you build self-trust, everything shifts:

- You no longer need sudden bursts of motivation, you act because it's who you are.

- Minor failures no longer terrify you, they're simply part of the process.

- You stop idolizing someone else's momentum and instead nurture your own.

You're not chasing an entirely new life, you're living out a new identity.

And that inner strength is far more enduring than any external validation.

The Internal Pact

Eventually, accountability deepens beyond external check-ins and promises. It evolves into an internal contract. You don't stick to your promises because someone is watching; you uphold them because they are part of who you've become. That is true power. That is freedom. Self-trust isn't something you can purchase; it's built, choice by choice.

REFLECTION:

Grab your journal and ask yourself:

- What promises have I made to myself that I've broken?

- When have I felt the most proud of who I am this year?

- What kind of person keeps going even when no one claps?

Write with complete honesty, no filters. This isn't about chastising yourself for the past but choosing how you appear next.

Reminder: You're not chasing perfection; you're cultivating a rhythm.

This rhythm outlasts fleeting motivation and, over time, transforms you into someone who needs no external validation to act. You become your own evidence.

Accountability Isn't Optional; It's the Blueprint for Your Future

Here's an unglamorous truth: You don't craft a new life with sudden breakthroughs; you build it through consistent, sometimes tedious, yet beautiful follow-through. That meeting you dreaded but still attended, that habit you maintained even when unnoticed, that tiny promise you kept to yourself instead of quitting: these are your building blocks. They are the invisible, irreplaceable moments that construct a future worth waking up to. Every ambition and every life you envision require solid infrastructure, not fantasies or grand declarations but frameworks, anchors, and systems. At the heart of that structure is one key element: Accountability. Not the kind born of punishment or guilt, but the kind that proclaims, "I show up because this is who I am." This form of accountability liberates you. When you know you're someone who honors their word to yourself and others, you're no longer a casualty of moods, distractions, or temporary storms. You become steady. You become inevitable.

The Crossroads

Right now, you stand at a fundamental crossroads: You can continue bargaining with your excuses, Or you can start building undeniable proof that you are becoming the person you promised to be. There's no magic solution, no perfect moment when everything aligns perfectly, only one option: You decide, and then you move.

Final Reflection & Pact

1. What single promise will you make and share today?

....

....

2. Who will you invite into your accountability circle?

....

....

Write your pledge in two sentences, for example:

"I will report my weekly progress on [goal] to [person]. I choose momentum over excuses."

....

....

....

....

Sign, date, and read it each morning as proof that accountability isn't optional, it's your blueprint for the future.

Your Next Step

Set up your accountability today:

- Create a "Proof Stack" – a list of tiny daily evidence of your progress.

- Build your "Accountability Team" – even if it starts with just one person for now.

- Anchor your commitments to consistent rituals, not fleeting moods.

Not tomorrow, not when life settles down, right now.

You don't owe anyone perfection, what you owe yourself is progress.

And the future you envision? It's waiting on the other side of your first kept promise.

Go ahead. Make it real.

GETTING STUCK
ISN'T FAILURE.
REMAINING IN
THAT STATE IS.

CHAPTER 15

Get Unstuck, Stay Unstuck

I wish I could promise that once you close this book, shed your excuses, and start building habits and rituals that redefine who you are, you'll never hit a roadblock again. But that would be misleading. You will encounter moments of being stuck. You will lose steam. You will begin to doubt yourself all over again.

Maybe not today. Maybe not next month. But eventually, those familiar doubts will creep back in. The old habits will reassert themselves. Life might catch you off guard with stress, grief, or unforeseen challenges, causing your hard-earned progress to waver.

It's nothing personal; it's simply part of being human.

I learned this lesson the hard way. After my first big breakthrough, when I started making moves, established a rhythm, and began to get noticed, I convinced myself I had overcome it all. I believed I was now untouchable, that I'd finally fixed my problems.

Then, in the span of a month, everything fell apart. A project I'd poured my heart into was put on hold. A health scare in my family shook my confidence. Suddenly, all the plans I relied on seemed laughably insignificant.

I didn't immediately spiral out of control. Initially, I did what high performers tend to do, I powered through. I meticulously filled my calendar. I promised myself I could outrun the uncertainty.

Yet, momentum built on anxiety is unsustainable. Over time, cracks began to form. I stopped reaching out, stopped writing, stopped creating. Bit by bit, I withdrew into that familiar comfort zone of "waiting to feel ready again," even though it was just the same old trap under a new guise.

When you find yourself stuck, it doesn't feel like a brief detour; it appears permanent. You tell yourself that the spark has vanished, that the magic that carried you this far is lost. You overlook the fact that being stuck isn't a label on you, it's a signal.

It's a cue indicating that something needs to change, not everything, just a piece of the puzzle.

Stuck Is a Symptom, Not Who You Are

The most dangerous part of feeling stuck isn't the delay it causes but the narrative you start building around it.

Instead of seeing your stuck as just a temporary situation, you begin to view it as a reflection of your character. "I'm lazy." "I'm not cut out for this." "I must have been faking it all along."

But those thoughts aren't evidence of a character flaw; they're simply indications of a human experience. They mean your current system needs an upgrade. They signal that you've reached the limits of your present capacity, hinting that you're ready for a new kind of growth if you can dodge the spiral of shame long enough to recognize it.

The people who avoid staying stuck the longest aren't those who never face setbacks. They're the ones who see the warning signs early and choose to act instead of criticizing themselves.

They don't blow things out of proportion; they adjust course.

Perfection isn't needed to keep progressing. You require enough honesty to notice when you're drifting and the discipline to pull yourself back.

Not through guilt or self-punishment, but with clarity and a plan.

In the next section, I'll outline what I call your "Lifelong Emergency Action Plan", your personal lifeline for when you start slipping back into old patterns.

But before we dive into that, I need you to internalize this:

Getting stuck does not cancel out the progress you've made. It only does so if you let it paralyze you.

Every day you get back up, even if it's awkward or imperfect, reduces the power of that stuckness.

So what? Recognizing stuckness as a signal frees you to treat it like a GPS alert: time to reroute, not retreat.

Stuck isn't who you are. It's your cue to reroute, not retreat.

REFLECTION PROMPT: **UNPACKING YOUR STUCK STORY**

Jot down these questions in your journal, on your Notes app, or on the back of this book:

■   When was the last time I felt stuck?

....

....

....

■   What narrative did I tell myself about why I was stuck?

....

....

....

....

■   How much of that story was rooted in shame, and how much could be changed?

....

....

....

....

(Take a moment to write. Reflection isn't filler; it's the roadmap back to momentum.)

Knowing stuckness is inevitable, let's blueprint your personal rescue kit, because preparation beats panic.

The Lifelong Emergency Action Plan

You don't craft an emergency plan when you're overwhelmed. You do it when you're clear, grounded, and ready to be honest with yourself.

Because when you're in the midst of chaos, tired, anxious, and riddled with doubt, the worst time to devise a rescue strategy is during the storm itself. In that state, you'll opt for whatever seems easiest: procrastination, avoidance, blame, etc. In short, anything except taking action.

True resilience isn't about being superhuman. It's about preparing your system to support you when your emotions threaten to sideline you.

I call this your Lifelong Emergency Action Plan because it's not a one-time fix or something for a single season. It's the support structure you construct now so that you already have a way to respond whenever life tries to shove you back into survival mode.

This plan has three components:

1. A Stuck Signature

2. A Minimum Viable Movement

3. A Pre-written Permission Slip

Let's build yours right now. No procrastination. No "I'll do this later." Because delaying is where stuckness wins.

Step 1: Identify Your Stuck Signature

First, you must recognize what being stuck looks like because it's different for everyone.

Some people become frantic, filling their calendars with busy work to avoid challenging tasks. Others withdraw entirely, stop responding, and shrink their worlds to the bare minimum. Some over-research, over-plan, or over-justify.

As for me? I become overly meticulous. I create countless new schedules and project plans. It appears productive, but it's merely rearranging the deck chairs on a ship I refuse to steer.

Your Stuck Signature is the default way you avoid hard work.

Name it now, while you're clear-minded, so that when it reappears, you can recognize it as a signal, not a life sentence.

Step 2: Define Your Minimum Viable Movement

When you're stuck, your brain will lie to you, insisting you have to solve everything before moving forward. That's not true.

You don't need a detailed master plan to fix your entire life. All you need is to take one small step toward regaining momentum.

That's what Minimum Viable Movement means: the tiniest possible action that still counts as forward progress.

It might not seem impressive or public, and it might only be meaningful to you, but it's real.

Maybe it's writing one sentence. Maybe it's doing one pushup. Perhaps it's sending a single email, making one phone call, or moving one file to a new folder.

Action matters because it reactivates your sense of self faster than motivation ever will.

Write down your **Minimum Viable Movement** for moments when you're stuck:

- One action for your career

- One action for your relationships

- One action for your health

- One action for your creativity

Design each to be so simple that you can do it without overthinking.

For example:

- "Write 50 words with no editing."
- "Move for five minutes, even if I'm just pacing."
- "Text one friend, even if it's just 'hey, I'm here.'"
- "Sketch for 90 seconds without judgment."

This isn't about constructing your dream life right away; it's about kickstarting your engine.

Step 3: Pre-Write Your Permission Slip

You know those voices that appear when you're stuck:

The Critic: "You're a failure."

The Protector: "Don't risk it again."

The Ghost: "It's all pointless."

In those raw moments, you won't be able to outthink them.

That's why you need a Pre-Written Permission Slip: a brief note from your clear-headed self to the part of you that's stuck, granting permission to move forward despite the fear.

For instance:

"You can take a step forward even if you feel scared, imperfect, and uncertain. You don't need to earn your way back into progress; a single step is enough."

Write your message and keep it somewhere you'll see it often: a phone wallpaper, a notebook, or your mirror. When doubt and shame get loud, this will be your guide.

When stuckness strikes, you won't be waiting for inspiration; you'll have clear instructions.

Real-Time Course Correction

If there's one thing I want you to take away from this book, it's that you can adjust your course without destroying yourself in the process.

You don't have to spiral into negativity, narrate your own failure, or let a bad hour define your day, week, or even your life.

You can catch yourself mid-fall, recalibrate, and disrupt the negative story before it hardens.

Many people don't realize this because they've been conditioned to believe in all-or-nothing progress. If you slip, you're "off track." Miss a day, and you've "ruined everything." Feel weak, and you're "not disciplined enough."

All of that is false.

The reality is that slipping isn't failure, spiraling isn't inevitable, and being stuck isn't who you are.

It's merely a blip, a brief interruption. It only becomes permanent if you allow it to be.

The Moment You Notice, You Win

There is a brief moment, right after you realize you're slipping but before the shame piles on. That's your opportunity. If you catch this moment and take action, you can break the cycle of stuckness. The moment you notice procrastination, take a two-minute action. The moment you spot avoidance, send an uncomfortable text. The moment the Ghost whispers, "It's too late," pause to breathe, reset, and do something small. Not because you feel completely ready but because you refuse to feed the narrative that you're stuck. Every second you spend battling those thoughts can be used to build evidence of progress.

Micro-Rescues Over Grand Gestures

When stuck, your mind might tempt you with grand, sweeping ideas: "I need to change everything!" "I'll start fresh on Monday!" "I need an entirely new system!" Stop.

These grand plans are mere illusions. They provide a sense of control without demanding immediate action. Instead, cultivate a micro-rescue habit: small, immediate realignments without negotiation.

Micro-rescues could be:

- Closing those ten open tabs and taking a deep breath.

- Writing a rough first sentence instead of obsessing over an essay.

- Walking around the block instead of overhauling your entire fitness plan.

They're tiny course corrections in the moment.

You don't need a massive comeback; you need a pivot.

The Three-Second Rule

Here's a tool I want you to adopt and never let go of: the Three-Second Rule for Recovery. Whenever you realize you're stuck, spiraling, or stalling, give yourself three seconds to take any micro-action towards your goals. Not three minutes, nor three hours, just three seconds. Notice the thought, move, text, open your document, hit record, raise your hand, speak up.

Don't allow hesitation to take over; interrupt your mind with action.

It might feel messy, imperfect, and strange initially, but it's the quickest way to rewire your brain from that "I'm stuck" mode.

So what? Tiny pivots beat perfect plans. So pick one microrescue and use it the moment you stall.

Build Your Emergency Plan (Before You Need It)

One common mistake people make is waiting until they're completely stuck to figure out how to break free.

It's like waiting until your house is on fire to start researching escape routes. By then, it's too late, too chaotic, and too overwhelming.

The smartest strategy is to design your Emergency Action Plan now while you're clear-headed.

Because being stuck isn't a matter of if, it's when.

Design it now so that you already know what to do when fear, doubt, or those three inner voices start shouting.

At the core of your Emergency Action Plan should be:

■ One Micro-Rescue Action: What's the smallest, quickest thing that nudges you toward progress? (Perhaps a two-minute walk, sending a one-sentence email, or uttering one brave phrase?)

■ One Reminder Phrase: What can you say to cut through panic? ("This feeling isn't final." or "Progress speaks louder than fear.")

■ One Person: Who can you reach out to, a friend or mentor, who will ground you without judgment? Not to rescue you but to witness your journey.

That's it. Three anchors. Three lifelines ready at any moment.

You don't need to be invincible. You need to be willing to change course.

With your plan in hand, here's the mindset shift that makes it work every time.

You Are Always One Decision Away

I don't care how tangled you feel right now, how long you've been stuck in circles, how many journals you've filled, dreams you've postponed, or promises you've broken. You are always just one decision away from altering your trajectory. It's not about one huge transformation or completely reinventing yourself; all it takes is one step. It works like that. Not because you're magical but because you're capable of movement. Once you move once, you can move again, and again, and again. That's how you become unstoppable. Not by never getting stuck but by refusing to let yourself remain stuck.

FINAL REFLECTION PROMPT

Take a moment and answer these questions honestly before moving on:

■ When I get stuck, what narrative do I usually create? ("I'm lazy." "It's too late." "It must be perfect.")

....

....

....

■ What micro-action can I take within those critical three seconds?

....

....

....

■ Who will I reach out to if I start spiraling?

....

....

....

■ What phrase will I cling to when I forget my strength?

....

....

....

Write these answers down and keep them visible because when stuckness strikes, and it will, you'll have a roadmap back to yourself.

Closing the Chapter, Opening the Future

This isn't the moment when you suddenly become "fixed." There's nothing broken about you.

This is the moment you realize that the only thing standing between you and the life you claim to desire isn't about time, talent, or destiny.

It's about movement.

It's about steady, relentless, humble, and awe-inspiring progress.

You already have everything you need. You are not behind the curve. You are not powerless.

You are the architect of your life. You embody the evidence and the proof of what's possible.

Now, take that step and move forward.

THE JOURNEY OF A THOUSAND MILES BEGINS WITH A SINGLE STEP.

— LAO TZU

Your Life, Your Move

Every transformation reaches a point when the noise gradually subsides. Not because everything is suddenly perfect or clear but because the choice becomes undeniable: stay as you are or move forward despite the uncertainty. That very choice is before you right now. You might have thought that more information, another breakthrough, or another reminder was needed. But the truth is both simple and challenging: it isn't another life plan you need, but a new relationship with action.

For too long, you've circled your potential, dreaming of what could be and waiting for the fearless, certain version of yourself to appear. The reality is that this version isn't waiting in the distance. It's built incrementally, with every step you take despite your fears, with every small action that overcomes a grand excuse. This isn't about earning your future but living it now. All the excuses, hesitations, perfectionism, self-doubt, weren't flaws in you. They were survival strategies that once made you feel safe. But safety is not the same as truly being alive. Now, you're ready for something bigger. Not because you suddenly became "worthy" but because you were always capable. You needed to stop waiting for permission.

The Quiet Power of Choice

Here's why many missed real change doesn't feel triumphant. It feels small and inconvenient, like showing up on an ordinary Wednesday when no one's clapping. Change happens quietly, when you move forward while your inner critic grumbles, while your protective instincts urge delay, and when old doubts whisper, "Maybe later."

You don't have to silence those voices completely; you need to decide they no longer control your actions. And that decision can be made today. Not dramatically or loudly, but quietly, in a way only you may notice. And you will notice the shift inside, a personal revolution that refuses to let another day shrink around your fears.

This Is Your Move

You don't need a flashier plan or another motivational speech. You have everything you need to take the next step:

- You have the truth: that perfection is a myth.

- You have the framework: the REAL Method to guide you.

- You have a system designed to outlast fleeting motivation and out-maneuver fear.

- And most importantly, you have yourself: imperfect, capable, and ready enough.

So what? All the frameworks in the world mean nothing until you take your first imperfect step, so let's make that move now.

Get Out of Your Own Way. You don't need another life plan; you need to stop standing in your own path. Every excuse you've leaned on was once a survival trick, not a roadblock. Now it's time to swap "I'm not ready" for "I'm choosing to move."

Sell Your Own Ticket. No one will hand you the life you want. If there's no seat, build one. If there's no opening, create it. Your future self isn't waiting for permission, they're waiting for your move.

REFLECTION & FIRST STEP

1. What permission have you been waiting to grant yourself?

....

....

....

....

2. What's one imperfect action you can take in the next five minutes?

....

....

....

....

....

Write it down, set a timer if you need to, and then do it, because momentum isn't built in thought but in movement.

Your journey begins now.

Final Word:

Let this moment serve as the first solid step in your new journey. Not because you're fearless or fully ready but because you've made a decision.

Take that step.

Notes

1. Walt Disney, quoted in *The Quotable Walt Disney*, ed. Dave Smith (New York: Disney Editions, 2001), 37.

2. Margaret Mead, quoted in *The World Ahead* (Washington, DC: U.S. Government Printing Office, 1960), 10.

3. Pauline R. Clance and Suzanne A. Imes, "The Impostor Phenomenon in High Achieving Women: Dynamics and Therapeutic Intervention," *Psychotherapy: Theory, Research & Practice* 15, no. 3 (1978): 241–47.

4. Lisa Feldman Barrett, *How Emotions Are Made: The Secret Life of the Brain* (Boston: Houghton Mifflin Harcourt, 2017), 52.

5. Rainer Maria Rilke to Franz Xaver Kappus, 16 July 1903, in *Letters to a Young Poet*, trans. Stephen Mitchell (New York: Vintage, 1986), 35.

6. Charles Duhigg, *The Power of Habit: Why We Do What We Do in Life and Business* (New York: Random House, 2012), 19–20.

7. Norman Doidge, *The Brain That Changes Itself: Stories of Personal Triumph from the Frontiers of Brain Science* (New York: Penguin, 2007), 125.

8. Carol S. Dweck, *Mindset: The New Psychology of Success* (New York: Random House, 2006), 6–7.

9. Albert Bandura, *SelfEfficacy: The Exercise of Control* (New York: W. H. Freeman, 1997), 36–37.

10. Wendy Wood and Dennis Rünger, "Psychology of Habit," *Annual Review of Psychology* 67 (2016): 289–314.

11. B. J. Fogg, *Tiny Habits: The Small Changes That Change Everything* (Boston: Houghton Mifflin Harcourt, 2019), 14–15.

12. Emma Grede, interview by Alexandra Sternlicht, "How Emma Grede Built a BillionDollar Fashion Empire with Good American," *Forbes*, October 5, 2021, https://www.forbes.com/sites/alexandrasternlicht/2021/10/05/how-emma-grede-built-a-billion-dollar-fashion-empire-with-good-american/.

13. Brené Brown, *Daring Greatly: How the Courage to Be Vulnerable Transforms the Way We Live, Love, Parent, and Lead* (New York: Gotham, 2012), 34.

14. Peter Lopez Jr., quoted in *The Relentless Mindset* (Chicago: North Loop Press, 2020), 112.

15. Walt Disney Studios, "Walt Disney Biography," Walt Disney Archives, accessed March 15, 2025, https://d23.com/walt-disney.

16. Maya Angelou, interview with Bill Moyers, "Facing Evil," *PBS*, February 14, 1988.

17. Michelle Obama, *Becoming* (New York: Crown, 2018), 389.

18. James Clear, *Atomic Habits: An Easy & Proven Way to Build Good Habits & Break Bad Ones* (New York: Avery, 2018), 25–27.

19. Walter Isaacson, *Steve Jobs* (New York: Simon & Schuster, 2011), 17–18.

Index of Frameworks & Strategies

ACKNOWLEDGMENTS

Writing this book has been one of the most vulnerable and transformational acts of my life. What began as scattered journal entries and late-night reflections took shape through the insight, accountability, and generosity of others.

I'm deeply grateful to the mentors, coaches, and editors who challenged my thinking, strengthened my voice, and helped bring this vision into focus. Your steady guidance gave this work its structure, urgency, and depth.

To my family, thank you for your unwavering belief in me. Your quiet strength and support have carried me through every phase of this journey. This book exists because of each of you.

ABOUT THE AUTHOR

Mary Ajayi is an entrepreneur, cybersecurity executive, and transformative coach recognized for helping ambitious professionals move with clarity and confidence. Her expertise lies at the intersection of governance, risk management, and personal growth, guiding high achievers from overthinking to decisive action.

She holds a Master of Engineering in Cybersecurity from George Washington University and completed executive education in Chief Information Security Officer (CISO) leadership at Carnegie Mellon University. With experience leading global security initiatives, launching high-impact education platforms, and shaping ethical frameworks for AI systems, Mary brings both technical precision and emotional intelligence to every project she leads.

She is the founder and CEO of a technology venture and the creator of Cyfendry Academy, a modern learning center where emerging leaders develop practical skills, strategic insight, and the resilience needed to thrive in high-stakes careers.

Mary is intentionally multifaceted. She is a builder, a teacher, a mother, and now, an author. Her debut book, *You're Not That Special,* is a direct, action-driven guide for high-functioning overthinkers who are ready to stop stalling and start moving.

She lives in the U.S. with her family and continues to lead, write, and coach with one core belief: clarity is power, but only if you act on it.

Learn more at **www.maryajayi.com**

Connect on Instagram **@notthatspecialbook**

www.ingramcontent.com/pod-product-compliance
Lightning Source LLC
Chambersburg PA
CBHW021717120626
46545CB00004B/1602